A Better Justice?

LAW AND SOCIETY

Law and Society Series
W. Wesley Pue, Founding Editor

We pay tribute to the late Wes Pue, under whose broad vision, extraordinary leadership, and unwavering commitment to socio-legal studies our Law and Society Series was established and rose to prominence.

The Law and Society Series explores law as a socially embedded phenomenon. It is premised on the understanding that the conventional division of law from society creates false dichotomies in thinking, scholarship, educational practice, and social life. Books in the series treat law and society as mutually constitutive and seek to bridge scholarship emerging from interdisciplinary engagement of law with disciplines such as politics, social theory, history, political economy, and gender studies.

Recent books in the series:

Trevor C.W. Farrow and Lesley A. Jacobs, eds., *The Justice Crisis: The Cost and Value of Accessing Law* (2020)

Jamie Baxter, *Inalienable Properties: The Political Economy of Indigenous Land Reform* (2020)

Jeremy Patrick, *Faith or Fraud: Fortune-telling, Spirituality, and the Law* (2020)

Obiora Chinedu Okafor, *Refugee Law after 9/11: Sanctuary and Security in Canada and the United States* (2020)

Anna Jane Samis Lund, *Trustees at Work: Financial Pressures, Emotional Labour, and Canadian Bankruptcy Law* (2019)

Shauna Labman, *Crossing Law's Border: Canada's Refugee Resettlement Program* (2019)

Peter McCormick and Marc D. Zanoni, *By the Court: Anonymous Judgments at the Supreme Court of Canada* (2019)

For a complete list of the titles in the series, see the UBC Press website, www.ubcpress.ca.

A Better Justice?

Community Programs for Criminalized Women

AMANDA NELUND

UBCPress · Vancouver · Toronto

29 28 27 26 25 24 23 22 21 20   5 4 3 2 1

Printed in Canada on FSC-certified ancient-forest-free paper (100% post-consumer recycled) that is processed chlorine- and acid-free.

Library and Archives Canada Cataloguing in Publication

Title: A better justice? : community programs for criminalized women / Amanda Nelund.
Names: Nelund, Amanda, 1985– author.
Series: Law and society series (Vancouver, B.C.)
Description: Series statement: Law and society | Includes bibliographical references and index.
Identifiers: Canadiana (print) 20200288334 | Canadiana (ebook) 20200288547 | ISBN 9780774863629 (hardcover) | ISBN 9780774863643 (PDF) | ISBN 9780774863650 (EPUB) | ISBN 9780774863667 (Kindle)
Subjects: LCSH: Female offenders—Services for—Manitoba—Winnipeg. | LCSH: Female offenders—Rehabilitation—Manitoba—Winnipeg. | LCSH: Female offenders—Manitoba—Winnipeg—Social conditions.
Classification: LCC HV9310.W56 N45 2020 | DDC 364.3/7409712743—dc23

Canada

UBC Press gratefully acknowledges the financial support for our publishing program of the Government of Canada (through the Canada Book Fund), the Canada Council for the Arts, and the British Columbia Arts Council.

Printed and bound in Canada by Friesens
Set in Bodoni and Baskerville10Pro by Apex CoVantage, LLC
Copy editor: Joanne Richardson
Proofreader: Amy Jackson
Cover designer: Gerilee McBride

UBC Press
The University of British Columbia
2029 West Mall
Vancouver, BC V6T 1Z2
www.ubcpress.ca

Contents

Acknowledgments

THIS BOOK HAS been awhile in the making and there are many people who have made it possible. To begin I would like to thank all of the women and men who participated in this research. Staff at community social service agencies have more than enough work to do without assisting researchers like myself. Despite that fact, many people took time from their busy schedules to sit and talk to me about their work. I hope there is something that they can take from my analysis to support and strengthen the work that they do.

I feel quite fortunate to work within what is a small but very vibrant community of critical criminology in Canada. This work was presented at several Critical Perspectives conferences. We have created a space in which critical criminology can grow and develop without constantly having to justify itself. This book emerges from many conversations in this community, and I hope can now add to those conversations. Thanks go to Debra Parkes, Rick Linden, and Elizabeth Comack for their feedback and encouragement. A special thank you to Andrew Woolford. Andrew's commitment to critical and socially just research has been, and continues to be, an inspiration. It was Andrew who convinced me that the ideas in *A Better Justice?* were worth sharing; thus, in so many ways, he is the one who made this book possible.

A Better Justice? was written as I joined and settled into the Department of Sociology at MacEwan University. This department is full of wonderful colleagues and students who helped me refine some of the ideas in the book. A special thank you to colleagues who read and commented on portions of the manuscript, whose commitment to thoughtful and critical scholarly work continues to inspire me, and whose care has been vital to building a scholarly career. Thank you to Kalyani Thurairajah, Alissa Overend, and Joanne Minaker. This book was supported by funding from the Office of Research Services at MacEwan University, as well as UBC Press, the Social Sciences and Humanities Research Council of Canada, and the University of Manitoba.

Thank you to Randy Schmidt at UBC Press for seeing and helping to realize the potential in this manuscript and for walking a new author through the process. Many thanks to two anonymous readers of the manuscript: this book is stronger because they generously took the time to read it very carefully. Thank you to the production team at UBC Press for helping to turn this manuscript into a book.

Finally, a warm thank you to all of my family and friends. Social and mental well-being are crucial to professional success, and they have all made sure I am well taken care of. In particular, as always, and by no means sufficiently, thank you to my husband Fraser. A thank you also to my daughter Abi. She is an inspiration for all of my work and for all of my attempts to create a more just world for her and those who follow us.

A Better Justice?

Introduction

IN TWENTY MINUTES, you can drive past all six of the community agencies in Winnipeg that offer justice services to criminalized women. The agencies – Onashowewin, Mediation Services, the Salvation Army, the Elizabeth Fry Society of Manitoba, the Native Women's Transition Centre, and New Directions – are located in the downtown and North End of Winnipeg. They are housed in nondescript buildings. Their foyers are similar: posters advertise legal aid and pardon services, positive parenting programs, public health announcements about being "With Child, Without Alcohol," and community events. Many have Indigenous art hanging on the walls, and at two of the sites the smell of sweetgrass is strong as they are spaces in which smudging takes place. I visited these agencies to learn about alternative justice: justice programs and practices that exist outside the formal structure of the criminal justice system. What kinds of justice practices are available for criminalized women in the community? What kind of work is done in these community spaces? What alternative to the formal justice system do they offer to criminalized women?

A Better Justice? explores the possibility of doing justice differently. It provides a close examination of alternative justice programs for criminalized women. I detail the types of programs available for criminalized women in Winnipeg, Manitoba, a midsize city in the Canadian Prairies, and analyze the kinds of work done by the agencies' programs as well as how staff think about the women with whom they work. The analysis focuses on the discourse constructed by alternative program staff and is accomplished through a detailed study of interview transcripts and program documents. I focus on the potential and the risks that lay in alternative forms of/approaches to justice. The decision to examine both the possibility and the danger of alternative justice comes from my bridging of two bodies of literature: feminist and criminological. Feminist criminologists have clearly detailed the need for alternative justice practices for criminalized women. It is from their critique of the justice system that I derived a sense of urgent need when visiting the community-based justice agencies. Critical criminological scholars, however, remind us that imagining and practising alternatives is not an easy task, and it is due to their literature that I retained a sense of scepticism as I sat in agency lobbies. Critiques of alternative justice complicate any straightforward claims that community alternatives are perfect solutions to criminal justice problems. This book begins by outlining both the feminist literature and the criminological literature that inspired the mixed hope with which I began this project. Feminist critiques of imprisonment makes clear the need for imagining and practising justice in new ways, while criminological critiques outline serious cautions that should be heeded with regard to alternatives. Throughout, I explore what is currently being done in the community for criminalized women and how alternative programs may do justice differently.

Women and the Formal Criminal Justice System

In 1990, the Task Force on Federally Sentenced Women released its report, *Creating Choices*, which included envisioning a "time when harm done to people will be repaired in creative, supportive, non-incarcerative ways" (TFFSW 1990, 104). The decades since have seen feminist scholars and advocates work tirelessly to critique the use of prison for women and to get women out of carceral institutions. Yet today women are the fastest-growing incarcerated population in Canada. Between 2005 and 2015, the federal prisoner population grew by 10 percent overall, while during that same period the number of women in federal custody increased by over 50 percent (Office of the Correctional Investigator 2015). Since 1995, the number of women in remand has doubled (Kong and AuCoin 2008). Indigenous and other racialized women have even higher rates of incarceration;[1] the number of Indigenous women in federal custody has gone up from 159 in 2006–07 to 251 in 2015–16 (Public Safety Canada 2017). Indigenous women make up over one-third of federally sentenced women, and yet Indigenous people comprise only 4 percent of the general Canadian population (Office of the Correctional Investigator 2015). This trend fits into a larger global pattern that sees women, particularly women occupying positions of complex social marginalization, incarcerated in growing numbers (Sudbury 2005).

Feminists have revealed the myriad ways that the formal justice system, particularly in the form of jail or prison, harms women. While prisons are inherently violent institutions, they have many unique impacts on women. Strip searches, while intrusive for anyone, take on a more violent meaning for women who have been sexually assaulted (Kilty 2014; Loucks 2004). As they are often sole caretakers of children, women risk losing custody when incarcerated (see the contributors to Minaker and Hogeveen [2015b] for more on criminalized mothers). Women prisoners spend more time in segregation than men (Balfour and Comack 2014), despite the fact that segregation has been shown to increase instances of self-harming behaviour (Kilty 2012, 2006; Martel 2000) and has been condemned by the Office of the Correctional Investigator (2017, 63) as "not an appropriate environment for women who are under observation for mental health problems, especially suicidal or self-harming ideations." Prison staff and policy often frame mental health needs and the "disruptive" behaviour that follows, such as self-harm and security issues, and respond to it with different forms, and higher levels, of penal control (Hannah-Moffat and Klassen 2015). Chartrand (2015) details the various forms of violence women encounter in prison and argues that the institution itself creates the conditions for violence and conceals the violence it produces.

Not only have feminists been critical of the harms women suffer while in prison, they also argue at a more fundamental level that prison is an inappropriate response to most women who commit crime. Feminists point to the social marginalization of female offenders and the causal role that this marginalization plays in their criminal offending. Most women are incarcerated for nonviolent property offences. Criminalized women are generally young, poor, and under-educated (Comack 2014; Johnson and Rodgers 1993). Feminist research into the pathways to crime and prison for women shows the impact of addiction and poverty (Balfour 2014; Comack 2014; Johnson and Rodgers 1993). Prison is not, according to feminist analyses, the way we should be responding to criminalized women. Their criminal behaviour is merely a symptom of their social marginalization. It is their marginalization that is the problem, and that is not something that prison can address; rather, it is something that prison often exacerbates.

Furthermore, many feminists have stressed the victimization history of female offenders. The 2014–15 report from the Office of the Correctional Investigator found that, of all federally sentenced women, 68 percent report being sexually abused and 86 percent report a history of physical abuse (Office of the Correctional Investigator 2016). This history can show up in women's subsequent incarceration, as years of feminist criminology has made apparent. Faith (1993, 106) names this phenomenon the "victimization-criminalization continuum." Comack (1996) illuminated the clear connections between criminalized women's histories of abuse and their criminal behaviour through her interviews with twenty-four women incarcerated in Manitoba's provincial jail for women. She concluded that, "once the connections are drawn between women's abuse histories and their troubles with the law, then it would seem relevant to query whether their incarceration serves any *benefit* – to the women themselves, to their families, to their communities or to the larger society" (126, emphasis in original). In her latest research, Comack (2018) returns to the provincial jail in Manitoba to explore whether the connections she saw in the mid-1990s are still apparent. For *Coming Back to Jail*,

Comack interviewed forty-two women and found that the experience of violence is still a key aspect of criminalized women's lives. In some cases, victimization has direct ties to offending behaviour, for example, in cases of self-defence; in others, it may be that alcohol and other drugs are used to cope with the victimization, and the use of these (often illegal) substances leads to criminalization. Faith (1993) emphasizes that there is not a deterministic relationship between victimization and criminalization but, rather, that social inequality creates groups that are harmed and that become the targets of selective criminal justice practices. It is often the case that both victimization and criminalization are outcomes of inequality.

Women's marginalization and victimization based on gender is, of course, complicated and compounded by other markers of difference. A feminist perspective that considers gender alone risks obscuring the unique experience of many women, but of particular relevance here is the experience of Indigenous women. The Canadian criminal justice system often responds disproportionately severely to Indigenous women. In 2014–15, Indigenous women made up 31 percent of federally incarcerated women and 38 percent of women sentenced to provincial and territorial custody. This overrepresentation is even more pronounced in the Prairie provinces. In 2008–09, Indigenous women made up 12 percent of the general Manitoban population but accounted for 85 percent of women sentenced to provincial corrections (Mahony 2011). The number of Indigenous women in prison in Canada has more than doubled since 2004 (Office of the Correctional Investigator 2014). Indigenous women (and men) are disproportionality placed in the maximum-security designation (Wesley 2012). Colonization and the patriarchal relations that structure colonial discourses and practices have created a situation of complex marginalization for Indigenous women, and it is within this context that their criminalization occurs (Fontaine 2014; Monture-Angus 1999). For Indigenous prisoners, prison in many ways mirrors the racist social context of the outside world. A Public Safety Canada report looking specifically at the conditions of prison and release for Aboriginal women offers this conclusion:

> To date, the experience of Aboriginal women in Federal penitentiaries has been a continuation of the marginalization experienced by generations of Aboriginal women. Issues of isolation and dislocation are commonplace for Aboriginal women across the continuum of Federal Corrections. Aboriginal women find themselves overrepresented in higher security classifications; overrepresented in Management Protocol status; they are frequently denied access to culturally and gender appropriate programming and as a group they are underrepresented in terms of parole eligibility. (Wesley 2012, 46)

For Indigenous women, all aspects of the prison experience are racialized.

In order to understand the justice system's treatment of Indigenous women it is imperative to understand Canada as a settler colonial nation. Settler colonial theory argues that settler colonialism is not a past event but, rather, an enduring and contemporary structure (Wolfe 1999). It is a structure in which Indigenous populations are removed from the land through a wide variety of discursive, practical, and violent moves (Veracini 2010). While it is not my intent to focus on settler colonial history, I highlight two manifestations of colonialism in Canada. These are practices that have clear gendered implications, and it is nearly impossible to think about the criminalization of and justice for Indigenous women without considering the concrete practices of settler colonialism. One of these practices is the apprehension of Indigenous children from their families and communities throughout history; the other is the victimization of Indigenous women, most dramatically seen in the number of women and girls who are missing and/or have been murdered.

One way in which settler colonialism has consistently attempted to extinguish Indigenous people has been through removing children from their families. This was done historically through the

Indian residential school system. This system, which operated from the early 1880s to the late 1990s,[2] saw over 150,000 Indigenous children taken from their families and communities and placed in schools that strove to assimilate them. Children at the schools were not allowed to speak their languages; they were taught that their cultures were inferior, and they suffered physical and sexual abuse. Although these schools no longer exist and the Indian Residential Schools Settlement Agreement was reached in 2006, the legacy of residential schools continues to affect individuals, families, and Canadian society in general. The "Sixties Scoop" was another widespread incident of child apprehension that occurred in Canada. This phenomenon is only beginning to be brought to the general public's attention, with class action lawsuits launched in several provinces. The term "Sixties Scoop" refers to a period from approximately 1960 to the 1980s in which Indigenous children were removed in large numbers from their families and placed in predominantly non-Indigenous foster and adopted homes. Many advocates and scholars frame the contemporary situation in Canada as a continuation of residential schools and the Sixties Scoop. Currently, in Manitoba, the majority of children in Child and Family Services (CFS) care are Indigenous (Hughes 2013). There are more Indigenous children in care now than at any point in history (Blackstock 2007, 2011). Indigenous children are removed from their families at higher rates than non-Indigenous children; they are more often removed for reasons related to poverty than to abuse; and child welfare services for Indigenous families are funded at a much lower level than those for non-Indigenous families (Blackstock 2011). These child removal practices are but a part of the larger settler colonial project in Canada.

Another way that settler colonialism operates in Canada is through violence against Indigenous women and girls. Somewhere between five hundred (NWAC 2010) and over eleven hundred (RCMP 2014) Indigenous women and girls have been killed or have gone missing in the last thirty years. Research conducted by the Native Women's Association of Canada (NWAC) documents many of the factors that place Indigenous women and girls in situations where their risk of victimization rises, including poverty, addiction, and survival sex work. The research carried out by NWAC also found, however, that simply being Indigenous is a dangerous situation for women in Canada. In a settler colonial state, Indigenous women are less valued than non-Indigenous women, thus violent men see them as easier targets and their cases are often treated less seriously by law enforcement and the courts than those involving non-Indigenous women. Families and advocates have been demanding the public's and government's attention to this issue for years. Over the past several years, all of the provincial governments in Canada, along with national organizations such as NWAC and the Assembly of First Nations as well as international organizations including Amnesty International and the UN Special Rapporteur on the Rights of Indigenous People, have called for a national inquiry into the issue. In 2016, the federal government of Canada set up an independent inquiry, the National Inquiry into Missing and Murdered Indigenous Women and Girls, to study and provide recommendations on the issue. At the time of writing, the inquiry is still doing its work and is not without criticism (see, for example, the Open Letter to Chief Commissioner Marion Buller 2017). My description of these practices is brief. I discuss them here in order to provide some context for the issues the participants in this study raise, and I encourage interested readers to look at the growing literature on all of these topics.

Child apprehension, violent victimization, and the myriad other practices and events that make up settler colonialism in Canada have led to high levels of social marginalization for Indigenous people. The colonial impacts on Indigenous people can be seen in stark relief in the Prairie provinces. Winnipeg has the largest Indigenous population of any major Canadian city. When compared to the non-Indigenous population in Winnipeg, Indigenous people are less likely to have completed post-secondary education and to have both lower incomes and higher unemployment rates (Urban Aboriginal Peoples Study 2011). In 2005, in Winnipeg over 40 percent of Indigenous people lived under Statistics Canada's low-income cut-off compared to 16 percent of non-Indigenous residents. This disparity is even higher for Indigenous children, 57 percent of whom lived under the low-income line compared to 20 percent of non-Indigenous children (Statistics Canada 2010). Brandon and Peters (2014) found that a number of factors, including legacies of colonialism, discrimination, and poverty, led to the high levels of homelessness experienced by Indigenous people in Winnipeg. The settler colonial context of Canada is crucial to understanding the criminal justice response to Indigenous men and women (see AJIC 1999). If we are serious about doing justice differently, then Indigenous women and settler colonialism must be at the core of our thinking.

Alternative Justice

When thinking about doing justice differently, of programming outside of the formal criminal justice system, it is tempting to frame these alternatives as "informal." Indeed, this is one of several different terms used to think about justice alternatives. Feenan (2002) begins his discussion of informal justice by emphasizing how hard it is to define; nevertheless, he goes on to define it as a non-state justice, based in the community. This is the way in which I framed the programs in Winnipeg as I began this research. One of my primary analytic tasks was to assess the degree to which alternative justice programs are informal or formal and to explore the meaning of this for staff. To that end, the project got off to an inauspicious start when, before the tape recorder had even been turned on, the first interviewee said, "I wouldn't call what we do here informal" (Hannah). In Chapter 1, I describe the various formal and informal elements of the programs. I want to note here that there are enough formal elements to the programs – formal relationships, goals, and practices – that labelling the work the agencies do as "informal justice" quickly begins to feel inaccurate. While no other participant challenged my use of the phrase "informal justice" as did Hannah, neither did any of them use it.

That being said, they did feel like they were providing something that differed from the formal justice system. So, unless referring specifically to the informal components of the programs, I use "alternative justice" rather than "informal justice" to describe these programs. I do so while acknowledging that this, too, is an imperfect label as it is clear at several points in the analysis that the community-based programs are very similar, in some ways, to what is offered in the criminal justice system.

The decision to use the phrase "alternative justice" is a theoretically important one. There is discursive power in the framing of something as "alternative," as Pavlich (2005) clearly demonstrates. He highlights the ways in which restorative justice has relied on contrasting itself clearly and forcefully to the criminal justice system. Advocates use a variety of themes "to distinguish themselves from criminal justice agencies by claiming unique objects, subjects, agents and processes to deal with criminal events" (13). Using the word "alternative" evokes a binary: it sets up the discussion as one that is naturally dealing with two opposing entities. Pavlich problematizes this binary theoretically by tracing the ways in which restorative justice relies on foundational criminal justice concepts even as it posits itself as an alternative to traditional criminal justice. In her study of what goes on at restorative justice conferences, Daly (2002) problematizes this binary empirically by showing the practical linkages between various "types" of justice. I try to avoid setting up this alternative justice versus criminal justice binary; however, I do use the term "alternative justice" as it reflects the participants' understanding of their work. Practically, I define alternative justice programs as those that are operated by a non-profit, social service agency and that provide any sort of direct services to criminalized women.

Restorative justice (RJ) is a particularly well studied and practised form of alternative justice, and it, too, has a variety of definitions. One of the most often cited comes from Tony Marshal (1999, 5), who defines restorative justice as "a process whereby parties with a stake in a specific offence collectively resolve how to deal with the aftermath of the offence and its implications for the future."

Although this definition gives a good description of the process of RJ, it implies that restorative justice is *only* a process. With this definition, restorative justice is being successfully practised if one is engaged in the correct form of mediation or conferencing. This is an inadequate conceptualization of RJ; indeed, there are a number of theories that animate and inspire the particular processes of RJ. Jennifer Llewellyn (2012) offers some of the most robust theorizing on restorative justice. She argues that it should work from a relational theory of justice. Restorative justice for Llewellyn is "concerned with responding to harms to relationships that flow from wrongdoing or that mark the existing structure of relationships" (104). While there may be disagreement about definitions, it is generally granted that RJ is a participatory, contextual, healing approach to justice (Woolford and Nelund 2019).

There are good reasons to believe that restorative justice and other alternative justice forms could be useful for criminalized women. Restorative justice has been described as a form of justice that gives conflict back to communities. This is typically done by drawing on the work of Nils Christie (1977), who argues that the state "steals" conflict from the direct "owners" or stakeholders and, in so doing, denies them the ability to participate and gain from conflict resolution. RJ becomes a way to empower communities to creatively solve their own problems. Others focus on the ability of RJ to inspire empathy and change in those who break the law (Braithwaite 1996; Sullivan and Tifft 2005). Victims, too, are seen to benefit as RJ may provide them with the space to forgive and to heal (Elliott 2011). In contrast to the formal system, wherein justice is delivered by professionals and punishments administered to little or no effect, restorative justice promises to engage those affected by crime, to build relationships, and to make lasting change.

I began my research by wondering if the community agencies in Winnipeg were fulfilling these goals for criminalized women. Perhaps, in their community offices, away from the justice system, alternative justice agencies are engaging in practices that create this type of justice – empowering, participatory, and community building. We can imagine that these non-profit social agencies are empowering individual women and creating supportive alternative communities. Perhaps they are centring women's voices and allowing them to narrate their own experiences and lives.

Any optimism I may have had that restorative justice, and other forms of alternative justice, could bring real change and justice to criminalized women was tempered when I examined non-feminist critical scholarly work. Critical criminologists are sceptical of the degree to which RJ and other alternative justice forms represent real alternatives. Stanley Cohen's (1985) classic book, *Visions of Social Control*, remains one of the most influential studies of alternative justice. Cohen argues that the effect of the psychiatric deinstitutionalization movement and the appearance of community control or community alternatives has not been to diminish the reach of the formal criminal justice system; rather, these alternatives have increased the number of people processed by the criminal justice system, increased the level of intervention, and supplemented rather than replaced the formal institutions. Social control, Cohen argues, is rendered invisible by, and stretches further into society through the use of, alternative programs.

Other scholars, coming from a different critical perspective, have reached similar conclusions. Restorative justice theory and programs have been critiqued for overemphasizing their difference from the criminal justice system. RJ programs are often "evaluated, vetted, approved, funded (wholly or mainly) and even initiated by state officials" (Pavlich 2005, 19). They receive participants via referral from the criminal justice system (Woolford and Ratner 2008). They are not discrete, separate spaces (which is how restorative justice theory often portrays them). Beyond these practical linkages, Pavlich (2005, 14) shows a deeper theoretical connection between restorative justice and the criminal justice system, arguing that "it is presented as a separate and autonomous entity; yet its foundational concepts derive from the very system it claims to substitute." These critics are pessimistic about the potential for restorative and other alternative justice programs.

Similar features have been identified by scholars who use the concept "penal voluntary sector." This work comes, primarily, out of the UK and examines the formalization of non-profit work and relationships with the state through changes to policy. Corcoran (2011) observes the ways in which non-profit organizations have been incorporated into the state and argues that this has meant that they begin to mirror the organizational structure of government and/or business. Tomczak (2017, 164) argues that voluntary sector involvement in policy reform was instrumental in creating a broader carceral reach as voluntary organizations' involvement "enabled and justified the further marketization and decentralization of penal services." The particular policy frameworks that Corcoran and others identify in the UK are not present in Canada; however, there are clear links between community agencies and the state.

There are not only practical and structural linkages between alternative and dominant justice work. One aspect of alternative, or voluntary, spaces that these literatures all identify is the potential for alternative spaces to reproduce dominant discourses. The potential for alternative justice to simply replicate, and in so doing to bolster, dominant discourses about criminalized women is a serious concern as feminist scholars have identified a variety of oppressive discourses in the criminal justice system. The predominant early mentality was one of paternalism/maternalism, according to which notions of ideal femininity, motherhood, and domesticity included the idea that women were naturally morally superior to men (Boritch 1997). This was reflected in the response of police, judges, magistrates, and other justice officials to women (Sangster 2001). These ideals also translated into middle-class female reformers arguing that, "if given a chance to bring their feminine influence to bear, they could redeem the fallen woman and make her into a 'true woman'" (Hannah-Moffat 2001, 29). Strategies of helping and protecting "fallen" women, including providing moral and religious teaching to female prisoners as well as training them to be good mothers, were put into practice. Indigenous women who were criminalized were seen as being in need of the same moral uplift as other criminalized women. This was seen as a necessary assimilative practice; however, it was also considered unlikely to succeed due to the "cultural inferiority" of Indigenous women (Sangster 1999). All criminalized women were incarcerated and supervised under the language of protection and assistance.

The criminal justice system has long responded to women based on social norms around gender, race, and class (Faith 1993; Minaker 2014; Sangster 2001), but the current strategies of neoliberal governance actually decontextualize criminalized women from their social context. Although neoliberalism, both in its general mode of governance and in its specific application to criminalized women, is explored more fully in the following chapters, I here provide a brief introduction for readers unfamiliar with the concept.

Neoliberalism is a ubiquitous concept that is defined and interpreted in many different ways (Larner 2000). Here it is examined primarily as a mode of governmentality rather than as a macroeconomic ideology or system, although these two understandings of neoliberalism are connected. In my usage, neoliberalism is a way of thinking about and enacting governance that centres on an active, responsible citizen and his/her ability to make good choices (Rose and Miller 1992). In the context of criminalized women, this has meant a significant shift from earlier maternalistic/feminist ideas that the state had a responsibility to rehabilitate or support women to the contemporary idea that "the offender is responsible for her own self-governance and for minimizing and managing her own needs and the risk she poses to both the public and herself" (Hannah-Moffat 2001, 172). When inequality is recognized as contributing to women's offending, the criminal justice system response emphasizes "the need for prisoners to rectify perceived defects within themselves" (Hayman 2006, 239). Although the response to criminalized women in Canada and in many other Western nations uses "gender-responsive" language, gender is seen as an individual trait, and there is a "slippage from gender oppression as a political and socio-economic structural force to one that is psychological" (Pollack 2013, 105). The responsibility lies with the individual woman to change her behaviour and make better choices (Hannah-Moffat 2001; Kemshall 2004).

In light of these serious problems, and others, feminist researchers and advocates have called for decreasing the use of incarceration for women. The feminist argument against the formal justice system is twofold: (1) a criminal justice response is unnecessary, in most cases, as feminist research shows women's criminal behaviour is a manifestation of their social marginalization, and (2) prison mirrors and compounds this marginalization. Feminist researchers argue that criminalized women must be situated and understood within their social context, that women's criminal behaviour can only be understood by confronting hetero-patriarchal, colonial, capitalist structures and discourses. As a corrective to the use of incarceration, many feminist scholars end their critiques of the formal system by calling for alternative justice programs.

Despite this recognized need for community alternatives, there is very little feminist research that looks at existing alternatives. *A Better Justice?* represents one of the few sustained analyses of alternative justice from a feminist perspective. We must know what is happening in the community in order to think and practise justice differently. On an empirical level, this book contributes to feminist criminology by outlining what justice programs exist for criminalized women. The main analytic focus is, however, on discourse. I examine how the programs think about criminalized women and alternative justice. I ask: Can alternative spaces of justice provide a way of thinking about and responding to criminalized women that is substantially different from that offered by the formal system justice? Do these spaces resist that system and broader discourses and practices of inequality? This is especially crucial in light of feminist analyses that demonstrate how the justice system can absorb feminist discourse and in light of critical analyses that demonstrate how alternative discourse can also be co-opted. I examine community programs for women but do so with some reservations about their potential. Critical criminologists have examined alternative justice and have shown the variety of ways that seemingly alternative programs reproduce and support the formal criminal justice system. In this book, I grapple with the clear necessity of providing alternative justice for criminalized women and the seeming impossibility of doing so.

A Foucauldian Feminist Analysis

I use the work of French poststructural philosopher Michel Foucault; however, I read his work through a feminist lens. Feminism is my primary epistemological, theoretical, and political commitment. As a feminist project, my research is motivated by an overarching commitment to end social injustice and oppression based on gender, race, class, sexuality, and other markers of difference. Prefacing "feminism" with "poststructural" or "Foucauldian" assists in locating my work within the wide and varied field that is contemporary feminism.

As mentioned above, my object of study is discourse, specifically the discourse created by community program staff. For Foucault, and poststructuralists generally, language is not simply a representation of reality; rather, it is the site of the construction of reality (Weedon 1997). Flax (1992, 453) argues: "to the degree that thought depends on and is articulated (to ourselves and others) in language, thought and the 'mind' itself will be socially and historically constituted." The knowledge we create is in turn constructed through language. The goal is not to get as close to reality as we can, not to uncover the *real* experiences or *real* people in our data, because we are unable to gain access to these in an unmediated way. Instead, the goal is to identify the ways in which social reality is constructed and experienced through discourse and associated practices.

Discourses are neither stable nor only produced as dominant: "discourse transmits and produces power; it reinforces it, but also undermines and exposes it, renders it fragile and makes it possible to thwart it" (Foucault 1978, 101). This is not to say that there is one dominant discourse and one resistant discourse; rather, we must view discourses as tactical elements that can be deployed in any number of ways. In analyzing the data used in this book, I pay heed to the multiplicity of discourses and their uses.

A key point of any feminist poststructural epistemology is that language is the site of both the construction of and resistance to social inequality. Weedon (1997, 40) defines poststructural feminism as "a mode of knowledge production which uses poststructural theories of language, subjectivity, social processes and institutions to understand existing power relations and to identify areas and strategies for change." A main tenet of this approach is that gendered identities are constructed in discourse. Those working from a feminist poststructural position argue that "it is language in the form of conflicting discourses which *constitutes us* as conscious thinking subjects and enables us to give meaning to the world and to act to transform it" (Weedon 1997, 31, emphasis added). This perspective focuses on how discourse is structured and on what power relations and subjectivities are produced and reproduced in the process. Throughout this book, I use a number of Foucault's concepts to analyze the power relations constituted through alternative justice discourse.

I begin from the feminist commitment to identifying, analyzing, and ending social inequality based on gender and intersecting power relations. I find Foucault's work, and the work of those feminists who have used it, to be indispensable. I utilize a governmentality framework to analyze alternative justice programs. In particular, I structure this book by using Foucault's concepts of power (Chapter 1), subject (Chapter 2), governance (Chapters 1 and 3), and resistance (Chapter 4). Foucault's ideas, however, are not unproblematic for feminists. One criticism that is shared by feminists who use his work (and by those who reject it) is that Foucault does not address gender, despite its seemingly clear relevance to his work, especially his work on sexuality and the body (Foucault 1978). This is not reason enough to dispense with his work entirely, but it does mean that, though I acknowledge the influence of Foucault's work, I often rely more heavily on feminist interpretations of it.

In examining the alternative justice discourse I ask of it the following questions: How do alternative justice staff position themselves in relation to the criminal justice system? How do they construct the criminalized woman? With what mentalities of governance do they respond to her? These are not questions of how they are *really* positioned, what they *really* do, or who the woman with whom they *really* work actually is. Instead, my concern is how all of these things are constituted in the discourses used by staff. This is important as it affects the ways they practise justice, seek and mobilize funding, and navigate relationships. So, while I do not study material practices and relationships, it is understood that these are not totally separate from discourse: they depend on each other.

A Note on the Research[3]

In order to gain access to alternative justice discourses, I interviewed staff at community-based social service agencies in Winnipeg, Manitoba, and collected a number of program documents. Six agencies were included in the research: Onashowewin, Mediation Services, the Salvation Army, the Elizabeth Fry Society, the Native Women's Transition Centre, and New Directions, all of which run a variety of programs for criminalized women.

The agencies range in terms of size and the scope of their program offerings. Some are local chapters of national organizations, while others are specific to Winnipeg. Both Elizabeth Fry and the Salvation Army are well-known Canadian organizations. The Elizabeth Fry Society is composed of local societies that "work with and for women and girls in the justice system, particularly those who are, or may be, criminalized" (see Canadian Association of Elizabeth Fry Societies at http://www.caefs.ca/). It has been doing advocacy and service-provision work for criminalized women since the first society was formed in 1939, and it has been a national organization since 1969. The Manitoba society is unique in that it describes itself as an Aboriginal organization. It runs a variety of different programs for all criminalized women in

Winnipeg. The Salvation Army is also a local chapter of a national organization. The Salvation Army is a Christian organization in Canada that works in a variety of ways to realize its mission to "share the love of Jesus Christ, meet human needs and be a transforming influence in the communities of our world" (Salvation Army website at https://salvationarmy.ca). It is within this context that the chapter in Winnipeg offers programming to women who work in the sex trade and men who avail themselves of that trade, and it runs a diversionary program for low-level offences.

The remaining agencies are local. New Directions is a large social service organization, and it offers a variety of programs that are categorized as counselling, education and training, or residential and support. The particular program that was included in this study is its Transition Education and Resource for Females (TERF), a program for women involved in the sex trade. Onashowewin is another local agency that self-describes as Winnipeg's only Aboriginal restorative justice agency. Unlike New Directions or the Salvation Army, Onashowewin is specifically focused on criminal justice services and provides restorative justice programming. Mediation Services is a Winnipeg organization that offers conflict resolution programs. My focus is on its Restorative Action Centre, wherein it provides restorative justice processes for crimes (however, it also offers non-criminal mediation). The final agency is the Native Women's Transition Centre, which has historically worked with women who are victims of violence. It offers first- and second-stage transitional housing and services. In 2011, it opened Kihiw Iskewock (Eagle Women) Lodge, a residential facility for criminalized women. In all of its residential sites and programming, the Native Women's Transition Centre strives to provide safe and supportive housing for Native women and children.

In order to study community alternatives, I conducted interviews with staff at the above-mentioned community agencies. Fifteen staff members, employed in various positions at these agencies, sat with me for in-depth, semi-structured interviews. These interviews constituted the bulk of the data for my book. I also gathered information ranging from internal program documents to website material and media reports. These data provided me with a wealth of in-depth, primarily descriptive information about the work being done in the community with criminalized women. My criteria demanded only that the agencies work with women, not that they work *exclusively* with women. Elizabeth Fry, Kihiw Iskewock's Lodge, and TERF work only with women, while the other organizations work with both women and men. All of the participants, however, made gender-based distinctions in their discussions with me.

Although I did not ask it of the participants, the majority, ten out of fifteen, self-identified as Indigenous. This is a demographic detail that must be mentioned in relation to the interview context as I am non-Indigenous, white, and Canadian, and feminist researchers are rightly concerned about how their social positioning, power, and privilege affect their research. In particular, feminists are sensitive to questions of identity and difference between themselves and their research participants. Much feminist research begins with a statement pertaining to the researcher's positionality. This is a laudable exercise in so far as it recognizes the social embeddedness of the researcher. It aligns very closely with poststructural arguments about power/knowledge and can allow researchers to reflect on how their power has shaped their research. However, even upon reflection, it is not always clear how the researcher's identity has affected her/his research. In her ethnographic research, Haney (1996) argues that this task was nearly impossible due to the multiple and sometimes shifting identity positions she occupied through the course of her fieldwork. Haney outlines the conflicting ways that her role as academic and, in turn, her age, gender, and class positioned her as a powerful outsider and an insider. She urges researchers to adopt an "understanding of reflexivity that recognizes the power dynamics of particular research settings" (776). As both researcher and participants hold a variety of identities, the impact of the various aspects of difference can change throughout any given interview.

Feminist researchers often position themselves by speaking to their power and the ways in which this may potentially constrain their data. The most striking impact of my identity was not how it silenced participants but, rather, the particular ways in which it incited them to speak. My identity as a settler Canadian led participants to offer information that they would not have offered had I been Indigenous. Hesse-Biber (2014) notes that being an outsider can mean the researcher asks questions that may have been taken for granted by an insider. During my interviews, without my asking, participants spoke to things that an insider would have taken for granted. They clearly articulated Indigenous issues in ways I do not think they would have done had I been Indigenous. They made sure to clearly connect the lives of the women with whom they work to colonialism. They did so in a spirit, I think, of teaching someone who does not have lived experience of colonial disadvantage or oppression and who has little knowledge of such. This assumption of my having no prior knowledge of the colonial context of Canada is not one they would have made of an Indigenous researcher. One participant went so far as to say: "I'll give you an example of what life can be like for a First Nations person ..." This is the clearest example of how the majority of the participants went to great pains to make race, colonialism, and their ongoing impacts on Indigenous peoples clear to me. The interviews are replete with this type of information. Perhaps these same participants would have spoken differently about these issues to an Indigenous researcher. It may be that they would have been able to speak in more complex ways to a researcher whom they felt shared their experience. But then again, perhaps they would not have spoken of these issues at all. This type of data may have gone unshared because there would have been no perceived need to teach an Indigenous researcher about the facts of colonialism. This dynamic helped to ensure that the analysis presented in this book keeps the experience of Indigenous women firmly in view.

Structure of the Book

A Better Justice? is animated by a desire to imagine justice differently. One step towards this is to assess the different ways that we currently practise justice. Throughout the book I examine alternative justice discourses in order to find promising directions for doing justice differently.

Chapter 1 focuses on the question: What alternative justice options exist in the community for criminalized women? I outline the various programs offered by community agencies in Winnipeg and argue that not only do these programs engage in alternative justice work, they also offer care, advocacy, and culture services to criminalized women. By examining the types of work the programs do, their various features, and their goals, I argue that they are neither entirely informal nor entirely formal; instead, they have elements of each type of justice. Using a governmentality framework and related literature, this chapter analyzes how the programs are being articulated into neoliberal government at a distance. Here we see both the potential for alternative justice to offer alternatives to criminalized women and the risk that these alternatives only amount to different ways of doing the work of the formal justice system.

Chapter 2 focuses on the subject of governance, and it looks at how staff and program documents constitute the criminalized woman. I outline the three main subjectivities found in formal correctional discourse: the neoliberal subject,[4] the psychologized woman, and the victimized (or what I prefer to call the marginalized) woman. Turning to the alternative justice discourse, I argue that the dominant subject positions are reconstituted with slight modifications. However, the dominant way in which the participants constitute the criminalized woman is different enough from how the criminal justice system constitutes her to allow the programs space to think about justice differently.

Chapter 3 analyzes the mentalities of governance present in the data. How do staff think about the work they do with criminalized women? Embedded in their description of their work is a strong neoliberal discourse on knowing and changing the self. Staff engage in a variety of practices that encourage criminalized women to become experts on themselves and to work to change themselves. Alongside this, however, is a clear ethic of care. In this chapter I argue that that these two governing mentalities interact in a contradictory manner, in some ways reinforcing neoliberal discourses and in other ways challenging them. The primary challenge I identify is the deployment and analysis of the techniques of the self that are offered to criminalized women as techniques of self-care. I argue that they fulfill many self-defined needs of criminalized women and assist in building capacity in women.

Chapter 4 brings my analyses together and assesses the degree to which the programs resist dominant neoliberal criminal justice discourses. I argue that there are a variety of strategies of resistance present in the programs that allows them to be spaces within which staff and criminalized women can resist. This resistance is both constrained and enabled by the programs' placement in the justice complex and their role as spaces within which women's lives and selves are governed.

The concluding chapter grapples with the questions addressed in this book and the questions that remain. I offer suggestions on how alternative justice can be practised so as to maximize its social justice potential. I also reflect on the role of critical scholars in assisting this endeavour. I summarize my analysis, speak to some of its limitations, and discuss its implications for both scholars and practitioners.

While feminist criminologists and socio-legal scholars have studied the law and corrections as spaces of governance for women, it is rare that they have looked outside of formal criminal justice institutions. Studies that have looked to community programs have tended to use theoretical perspectives that lead them to see the criminal justice system and neoliberalism as totalizing and as always co-opting any difference or resistance that may reside in the community. In *A Better Justice?* I analyze alternative justice programs to chart both dominant and resistant discourses in order to assist in conceptualizing how it is we may do justice differently with and for criminalized women.

I argue that the programs under study are not wholly alternative, that we must think of them as spaces of governance, which, in many instances, contain dominant criminal justice discourses. This is not to belittle the work that is being done by staff. Importantly, some of these programs are doing something radically different for some women: they are getting them out of carceral institutions. Elizabeth Fry's bail supervision program allows women to avoid being remanded into provincial custody. If not for this program, the women with whom staff work would be sitting in the Women's Correctional Centre waiting for their case to come before the court. Kihiw Iskewock Lodge allows women to serve a portion of their sentence in the community and, in doing so, helps them to come out of provincial jails and federal prisons. Though I argue that the distinction between informal and formal is nuanced, complex, and often overstated, for criminalized women this distinction can be stark. As Caitlin described it, it is a difference "in terms of custody and freedom," and, by participating in the program, "they can walk outside and breathe the fresh air." As someone who has always been able to walk outside, in my analysis I do not want to minimize the difference that the ability to do this can make to someone's life.

1

Alternative Work: Examining the Justice, Social, and Culture Work Offered by the Agencies

> I would just like them to take something. You know, whatever it is, if it's the friendship, if it's the fellowship, if it's the cooking. If it's the going out, the meeting new people, you know, going on adventures, doing all these things.
>
> (Staff member at Kihiw Iskewock Lodge)

> So, we're more restricted. We struggled with the whole feminist philosophy of helping and empowering women versus implementing an oppressive judicial system from which they are staying with us as a result. But the reality is, if we don't create safety and have them have an idea what it looks like ... So, we had to be more invasive and sort of waive our feminist approach to healing and also some things to ensure, again, is she safe? So it has changed how we operate absolutely. Just the training of our staff. For them to do room searches because that's very invasive and they've never done them ... It made us sort of tighten up a few things.
>
> (Staff member at Kihiw Iskewock Lodge)

In order to analyze how these alternative justice agencies may do justice differently, I begin by outlining what precisely it is that they do. The community agencies offer criminalized women an array of programs and services; the staff quoted above refer to just a few aspects of their work. Staff engage in both informal and formal justice work, social work,[1] advocacy work, and culture work. These are *my* classifications: the programs do not use these labels nor do they discuss their work by using any strong distinctions.

Separating these types of work from each other can assist us in seeing just what alternatives are offered by "alternative" justice. In this chapter, I describe the alternative justice programs that are available for criminalized women in Winnipeg and highlight the seemingly contradictory presence of both informal and formal practices, goals, and relationships. Though these are alternative justice programs, they offer surprisingly little alternative *justice* work. Rather than offering innovative ways of responding to harm, much of the justice work these programs do assists and mirrors what is done in the formal criminal justice system. The bulk of their alternative work is better thought of as social, advocacy, and culture work. Staff support the women in the programs, they advocate for them, and they engage them in Indigenous cultural practices and teachings. I use a governmentality framework to assist in making sense of this variety of practices and in analyzing the ways in which the programs both mirror and challenge criminal justice practices and discourses. Here I introduce that framework and use it to argue that alternative justice programs are key sites of government at a distance and are part of the informal-formal justice complex.

Alternative Work

The agencies do alternative work that is directly related to criminal justice. This work focuses on the women's offences, their status as "offenders," and the facets of their lives that are seen as direct precipitating factors in their offending. According to the Onashowewin website: "The approach of Onashowewin is to try and address underlying issues that have led to criminal behavio[u]rs and make the offenders accountable for their actions." While no other agency articulates this approach quite so directly, this captures much of the work they all do. There are three types of informal justice offered for criminalized women: restorative justice, educational or self-help programming aimed at responding to their offending, and reintegration services. Restorative justice is drawn on very broadly by the programs under discussion, viewed not as a particular form but, rather, as "a process to involve, to the extent possible, those who have a stake in a specific offense and to collectively identify and address harms, needs and obligations, in order to heal and put things as right as possible" (Zehr 2002, 37). Both Mediation Services and Onashowewin offer restorative justice programming.

All of Mediation Services' work with respect to criminal offences is restorative in nature as it facilitates victim-offender mediation sessions. Erika outlined the process:

> Well what mediation would involve would be the two parties coming together with or without support people. Sometimes people do request that they have someone there as a support person. All that [is] sort of negotiated ahead of time just so everybody is aware of who is going to be in the room. From there the mediators will set out the ground rules, kind of start the meeting. From there, hear from each person their perspective about what happened. From there they take a look at what the interests are. About the topics that need to be talked about. Once those are talked about and people have had a chance to discuss the impact the actions have had on them then we start looking at what needs to happen to move forward. What do you need to put this behind you?

In cases where the victim does not want to meet face to face with the offender, mediators can engage in shuttle mediation, bringing the concerns and story of each to the other and facilitating an agreement without a face-to-face meeting. For situations in which the victim is not at all interested in participating, Mediation Services offers a meeting between the offender and community volunteers, during which the impacts of and motivations for the harm can still be discussed. Mediation Services very strongly grounds the work it does in restorative justice literature and theory.

Onashowewin also practises restorative justice. Its mission is to "provide culturally based restorative justice practices to those in conflict with the law, while ensuring that healing occurs for those harmed and our society is safer through the prevention of recidivism" (Onashowewin website at http://www.onashowewin.com). It does offer victim-offender mediation; however, the bulk of what it does focuses on working solely with the offender in a restorative way through a variety of workshops. The two programs offered by Mediation Services and Onashowewin differ in the degree to which they can be situated within RJ programming and theory. Staff at Mediation Services referenced RJ scholars in their interviews and have degrees in mediation, peacebuilding, and other areas of restorative justice. Onashowewin draws broadly on themes of restorative justice, such as relationships and healing harm, but grounds itself more firmly in its Indigenous understandings of justice.

The second type of alterative justice work in which the programs engage is educational and personal development work related to the offence and the offender's background. Though participants noted low levels of formal education as a common feature of the women whom they serve, only two agencies offer programming to address this issue. Educational programming is offered by the Native Women's Transition Centre and the Elizabeth Fry Society. The Kihiw Iskewock Lodge mandates participation in either education or training for each woman who lives there. As a staff member at the Lodge described it: "Now there's the opportunity for you when you come in, you make a commitment to participate in one of those two streams. Education, training and trades or cooperatives. So, all of the women that are coming in are going to be able, I mean they have to do something." The Lodge offers high school credits and GED as well as post-secondary credits through a partnership with the University of Winnipeg. Elizabeth Fry offers literacy programming and assists with a teaching program in the provincial jail.

Some of the agencies also offer employment skills and training. Once again it is Kihiw Iskewock Lodge that offers these services in the most robust way. As part of its Education, Training and Trades stream, Kihiw Iskewock has partnered with BUILD, a "social enterprise non-profit contractor and a training program for people who face barriers to employment" (BUILD 2014). The Lodge also partners with SEED, an organization that provides "capacity building services that assist low-income individuals, groups, organizations and economically distressed neighbourhoods to improve their social and economic vitality" (SEED 2014). The Lodge has made education and training a key focus of the work it does. A staff member described the Lodge: "It's a full adult learning environment that we're in the process of building right now actually. So that's pretty exciting and that's what Kihiw Iskewock Lodge will do." Elizabeth Fry has computers at which women can work on their resumes or search for jobs. Though these are the only direct education or employment training offered by these agencies, many of the staff interviewed stated that exploring the education levels and employment situation of the women with whom they work is a regular component of their process. Andi, for example, included "how to get education. How to complete the education" in a long list of things with which the Lodge's reintegration worker assists. Similarly, Onashowewin agency material notes that, once it closes a file, it will still try to assist its clients by referring them "to additional agencies for housing, training, employment and education opportunities."

Last, and most common, the agencies under study offer personal development courses. These include several different anger management courses offered by Elizabeth Fry, Onashowewin, and the Salvation Army. Elizabeth Fry and Onashowewin both offer workshops on addiction and workshops on shoplifting.

In addition, many of the agencies offer their own unique personal development programming. Onashowewin's process for women (and men) who participate is to set up each individual with a variety of workshops. As one staff member put it: "Then we review the case, conduct an in-person interview, go over the consent form, release of information – are they status or not status – and construct a case plan. It's generally made up of workshops." Including the workshops mentioned above, Onashowewin also offers a women's workshop and a men's workshop. These are grounded in Indigenous knowledge and share teachings about the role and responsibilities of men and women. It also offers a workshop on healthy relationships. The combination of workshops given to an individual will depend on her offence and her needs, but there is one that all participants must complete. It is called Mino-Bimadiziwin, and it focuses on "making positive and healthy decisions and life choices" (program document).

The Salvation Army runs what it calls the Positive Lifestyle Program, which strives to "help people realistically face the consequences of their behaviour, begin to understand the relationship between the offence and emotional difficulties and learn to take responsibility for their actions" (program document). A variety of topics are addressed in this weekly, two-hour group session:

> It's really just general life skills things. It's a lot of self-reflection. We talk about things like stress management, self-esteem, assertiveness, conflict resolution, transition grief loss. Healthy relationships. Just a variety of different things ... and people go, "Wow I didn't, I didn't know about that" or "I didn't see that" (staff member).

The Salvation Army also runs a three-day camp for women involved in the sex trade. The camp offers "educational, therapeutic and recreational components" (program document), with the educational component comprising a workshop on the legal consequences of involvement with the trade, another on gaining access to community resources, and a third in which they learn about sex trade clients, or what is referred to as "John-ology."

New Directions' Transition Education and Resource for Females program has a classroom component. While it runs classes and offers credits, it is not educational programming that would be formally credentialled in the way that high school or post-secondary course offerings are. Instead, the classes are focused on general life skills, offering a credit in family studies and one in foundations of healthy living. Mediation Services, because of its focus on discrete conflicts and resolving the matter at hand, does not do any in-house programming. As part of the mediation agreement, however, individuals may be required to attend anger management classes or counselling.

The third type of justice work done by some of the agencies is reintegration services. The Native Women's Transition Centre houses and strives to reintegrate women coming out of provincial corrections, federal corrections, and drug treatment court as well as women with care agreements with CFS. Women can receive temporary release to the Kihiw Iskewock Lodge to serve the remainder of their correctional sentence. Kihiw Iskewock allows women to leave jail or prison and provides them with housing, services, and supervision.

The Elizabeth Fry Society has a bail supervision program that helps prepare bail plans for women who would not otherwise be able to secure bail. Once released to their care, they assist the women in various ways to help them reintegrate into the community. It also has a provincial reintegration worker who works with women coming out of the formal system after attaining bail or after having served a period of incarceration, and it assists with transitioning them back into the community. Reintegration services often include things as basic as assisting women to acquire identification and family doctors in conjunction with the educational programming mentioned above.

Formal Justice Work

Alongside offering informal justice programming, the agencies also engage in highly formal criminal justice work. Mediation Services, Onashowewin, and the Salvation Army all offer official diversionary programs. This means that either pre- or post-charge, the Crown will refer cases to one of these agencies. Direct referrals can be made to a specific agency such as Mediation Services when there is an identifiable victim, Onashowewin when the offender is Indigenous, or the Salvation Army when the offender is either the purchaser or seller of sex. Alternatively, the Crown can make a general referral for diversion, and the three agencies triage every week to go through cases and split them up. No matter the referral source, once an agency has the file a case plan is constructed, and it will look different depending on which agency develops the plan. Kirsten outlines the process:

> Then the agreement is drawn out and everybody signs it and they both get a copy. From there the case worker would monitor that agreement to make sure whatever is said there, make sure that happens. In the meantime, I tell the Crown attorney of, kind of, the progress of where things are at. If it's post charges then we'd be asking remand dates. You know, until they've completed what they needed to do. Once everything is complete then we make the recommendation for stayed proceedings. If they don't follow through then it gets referred back to court.

Another scenario in which a case will be referred back to the court occurs when the accused does not take responsibility. As Sarah explained, "If the individuals feel they are not guilty of the offence then they don't qualify to participate and we just suggest they go back through the court process." Operating as diversion programs, the agencies fulfill the case-processing function of the courts and corrections.

The Native Women's Transition Centre and Elizabeth Fry do direct supervisory work. Kihiw Iskewock Lodge is available only to "mandated women," who must come in with legal conditions, be it from a parole order, probation order, drug treatment court order, or CFS agreement. The Lodge is then responsible for the supervision of that order. Case managers "have their file, paperwork, expectations, if they're dealing with the province, they have to start taking notations, making monthly summaries for everybody" (staff member). There are curfew checks and women must sign in and out of the Lodge. Upon arrival at the Lodge, women are restricted to the facility:

> The first forty-eight hours they're locked in. Well, not locked in, it's a grounding. It's a really stupid word. They have to stay in the centre for forty-eight hours just so they can get used to the

> chores. Because there are quite a lot of rules here. It's not like you just get to come and there's your apartment and you get to go. It's communal living. (Staff member)

Staff discussed some of the security measures the Lodge had to implement: "So we have 24/7 staffed all our facilities. We have implemented room searches and belonging searches. We can access drug-sniffing dogs from Corrections. So, we've really cracked down on, because I mean it is what it is." Any breaches of the order are reported by Lodge staff and may result in a warrant being issued for the woman's arrest.

Elizabeth Fry offers similar supervision of bail plans, as outlined by one of the bail supervisors:

> Sure, how we do it right now, well how we've been doing it since the beginning of it was that a woman or the lawyer would contact us, the bail supervisor, and give the information to him and he would put it on the, put the woman on a waiting list. Then from there he would assign to myself or the other bail worker and we would go and do [an] interview with them. Which can last an hour and a half. Then we have to verify information, we have to write up a report, and also in the report we also write up a bail plan on, [things] such as programs they can, that we can help them attend, that we want them to attend. We also give them a curfew.

As well as constructing the various conditions for each woman, the bail supervisors engage in curfew checks, ensure the women are keeping to their conditions, and report any breaches. This involves considerable supervision, as noted by another supervisor:

> So, say they're living here, then it's much easier for me to check curfew because of our camera. Yeah. That's pretty easy. If they're at their own residence then yeah, I do surprise curfew checks. I do phone curfew, the whole bit. You know so it's, it's, I'm very involved in their life.

This bail program involves the criminal justice system directly contracting out an aspect of its work. One of the bail workers described the work as "basically Justice. This office is basically, in, I guess in a lack of better words, is Justice-owned. Anything I write and anything I do is Justice-owned. They pay for my position." In some ways, these agencies are conducting formal criminal justice business outside of typical criminal justice sites.

Non-justice Work

Alongside the justice programming offered by Winnipeg's community agencies is a variety of other types of work. Indeed, the work that can be classified as informal justice makes up a strikingly small part of the agencies' offerings. Staff engage in activities that fit within a broad definition of social work. Much of what my participants described could be grouped under the Canadian Association of Social Workers' definition of social work as a profession "concerned with helping individuals, families, groups and communities to enhance their individual and collective well-being." Participants spoke about assisting criminalized women with finding housing and other basic necessities. The focus of much of their work is on meeting women's needs and providing for their overall well-being. Julie talked about "looking again through a holistic model and how we help people to find themselves again and that balance." I speak at length about this type of work in Chapter 3. For now, it is sufficient to note that, although the agencies focus on *criminalized* women, their work is not limited to justice services.

Most of the participants also spoke about their advocacy work, which has two dimensions: personal advocacy for individual women and political advocacy for criminalized women as a group. Participants spoke about advocating for individual women within the justice system. Some, as Chris describes, would actively request a case for diversion:

> We go to court on a weekly basis for first-time charges. We listen to the dockets, go early, pay attention to people, try to notice

> anything out of the ordinary. We hang around and talk to people, ask them: "Is this your first appearance? What's going on? Do you have lawyers? Could it be diverted?" The problem is that young people, or older people for that matter, they don't know the process.

Other participants echoed this concern that most of their clients do not understand how the justice system works, even as they are being processed by it: "My breath is always taken away that even though they might have been involved in the criminal justice system since youth, and involved quite extensively, they don't understand the criminal justice system" (Emily).

Alongside justice system advocacy, many participants described helping women navigate the child welfare system and the social assistance bureaucracy. This included taking them to appointments, writing letters of recommendation, helping them to meet the demands of these systems, and, when necessary, challenging them. As Veronica explained with regard to CFS: "So we fought tooth and nail to have not one more child go into the system with attachment disorder because they took her away when they were a baby. So, we won that one. So, she's going to be raising her little baby." Participants also spoke about how, along with providing direct assistance, they taught women to be their own advocates.

The agencies also engage in broader group advocacy work. Elizabeth Fry's mandate includes advocacy, and it performs quite a lot of formal legal advocacy. It engages in tours of confinement in provincial facilities during which its members report any breaches of policy or law to the correctional investigator. Elizabeth Fry also brings Charter challenges to court and makes frequent public statements about issues related to criminalized women. Many of the other agencies also advocate for criminalized women (and men) in general. For example, in 2013 a local theatre company wrote and produced a play titled *Jail Baby*. It was written in partnership with the Elizabeth Fry Society, and, as part of its performance each night, a panel of speakers addressed different themes related to criminalized women. Representatives from every agency under study participated in that production. In 2014, Onashowewin and Elizabeth Fry hosted a public discussion led by then executive director of the Canadian Association of Elizabeth Fry Societies, Kim Pate, and Debbie Kilroy, the CEO of Sisters Inside, an Australian advocacy group for women in the criminal justice system. This discussion was held at Onashowewin's office and was highly critical of the way the criminal justice system oppresses women, particularly Indigenous women. Onashowewin and Elizabeth Fry also take part in Prisoner Justice Day, another public advocacy event. My knowledge of this comes more from my interactions and observations outside of the research context than from my data, perhaps because participants did not think of these events as work with women.

Alongside justice, social, and advocacy work, the agencies also engage in what I term "culture work." This is work that is done specifically in relation to Indigenous culture and identity. Indigenous women were seen by staff and programs as benefiting from a connection or reconnection to their culture in a way that no other group would. The Native Women's Transition Centre, Elizabeth Fry Manitoba, and Onashowewin are all Aboriginal organizations. The other agencies also, to varying degrees, engage Indigenous culture in their broader work. For some agencies, this means being able to offer traditional ceremonies to participants and staff:

> You can smudge anywhere here. There are some pipe carriers on staff so that if you wanted a ceremony, this year we're trying to have regular sweats because [for] a lot of the women it's about the culture. (Emily)
>
> We can hook up the women to Elders, and if they want to go to sweats, we can send them to sweats or we'll take them to sweats. Pipe ceremonies, our ED [executive director] is a pipe carrier. We'll do drumming here every now and then. (Kate)
>
> So, I invite them to talk about these things. See how they see it. Yeah. And sometimes we'll talk about the teepee and its meaning or we'll talk about the sweat lodge, how you offer

> tobacco. I'll talk about the four sacred medicines that were given to our people in order to cleanse ourselves. I'll talk about smudge, and why we smudge, and then I'll offer the smudge to each person in that circle and let them know I don't force them, but I'm offering. (Andrea)

Some agencies incorporate Indigenous perspectives into their programming. New Directions' Transition Education and Resource for Females program incorporates the medicine wheel into its general programming, while Native Women's Transition Centre focuses on the seven teachings. Onashowewin uses culture as the basis for all of its programming. As Ariel stressed: "Culture is the heartbeat of the program. It permeates the whole program, everything we do." Teachings about Indigenous cultures, perspectives, and histories are a part of all of Onashowewin's workshops. None of the participants spoke about culture in a way that would suggest that they limit it to the "justice" aspects of Indigenous culture. The agencies do not simply offer Indigenous justice; rather, they incorporate culture and culture work into all their programs.

These agencies contain many informal elements. They are non-profit community organizations. They are staffed by non-professionals: these are not lawyers or judges, they are laypeople. To add to their informal character, the agencies rely heavily on volunteers, do much of their own fundraising, and receive support from such community funders as the United Way and the Winnipeg Foundation. In some cases, the agencies have an open-door policy and take self-referrals from anyone who needs assistance. Staff engage in a variety of alternative forms of work. However, the agencies have a number of formal elements. While they take referrals from many sources, the clear majority of their cases come from the criminal justice system. They are funded, in many cases, by Manitoba Justice or the Correctional Service of Canada, and they perform criminal justice work. The alternative justice programs offered by these agencies are not spaces that are free of institutional power simply because they are located in the community rather than in carceral institutions.

The agencies and the programs they offer are neither free from power nor mere extensions of the formal justice system. This positioning affects the work they do. It affects what kind of work the staff does, and it leads them to see themselves both as alternative and as connected to the criminal justice system. The relationship between the agencies and the criminal justice system and the way staff think about their position cannot be reduced to an either/or relationship. However, the formal justice versus informal justice binary is one that appears throughout much of the literature on alternative justice. A simple definition of informal justice situates it as a form of non-state justice, based in the community (Feenan 2002). The formal justice system and informal programs are generally contrasted according to a variety of aspects: values, practices, theories, and actors. A primary way that much of the literature distinguishes between these two types or sites of justice concerns the presence or absence of power, which is also a common thread that runs through other differences. Informal justice, and the community in which it takes place, is portrayed in much of the literature as free from power (see Pavlich 2001 for an extended analysis). This is particularly evident in much of the restorative justice literature, where power is understood as primarily oppressive and as a zero-sum proposal: the state and the formal institutions of the criminal justice system have power while, conversely, the community and informal institutions do not. Walgrave (2002, 72) is critical of this trend in restorative justice thinking, arguing that, within the RJ literature, "community is then advanced as the social environment of informal interactions based on spontaneous human understanding, as opposed to the formal institutionalized society ('the government' or 'the state') with its rules and rigid communication channels." The extensive use of Christie's (1977) premise that the state steals conflict from individuals and communities demonstrates how much of the restorative justice literature sets up the state as an all-powerful thief and the community as an inherently positive space (see Elliott 2011).

A different, but related, tendency is evident in the social control and transcarceration literature. It, too, begins from the understanding of power as negative, repressive, and state-centred but then argues that, rather than being free of this power, informal justice is always subject to state power. This means that informal community programs are always seen as replicating state processes or as becoming "co-opted by and absorbed into the formal state apparatus" (Maidment 2006a, 127). Although useful for highlighting some ideal strengths and weaknesses of informal justice, both approaches risk obscuring the unique power relations present in informal justice programs. This framing leads to a tendency to set up informal justice and formal justice, and the criminal justice system and the community, as separate and distinct spaces that either remain untouched by each other or in which the state/system/formal dominates the community/informal. It leaves us with an either/or that is theoretically limiting and that does not fully capture the empirical reality of alternative justice.

Governmentality and Neoliberalism

I use the concept and literature of governmentality in order to complicate our understanding and avoid the problematic binary of informal justice versus formal justice and criminal justice versus alternative justice. This literature allows for analyses that do not necessarily conclude that alternative justice is all good or all bad. Governmentality analyses, following Foucault's (1991) now classic analytic of power as relational, productive, and dispersed, work to identify the practices and knowledges that govern our behaviour (Garland 1997). Analysts using this perspective focus on the ways in which power is exercised to create subjectivities, spaces for thought, and modes of acting. The focus is on government as any strategy or action that involves the "conduct of conduct" (Dean 1999). The conception of power as dispersed and of government as a broad strategy leads to an extended conception of governing authorities, one that includes actors such as community agencies and their staff. This wider group of authorities operates in different sites, with different technologies and mentalities (Rose, O'Malley, and Valverde 2006). Analyses using a governmentality perspective identify the authorities that are involved in an act of governance, the sites of governance in which they exist, their objectives, and their strategies of governance (Rose and Valverde 1998; Rose, O'Malley, and Valverde 2006).

Using a governmentality lens allows me to see alternative justice as a space in which power is exercised but may look quite different from what it looks like in the justice system. The power relations involved may be unique to alternative justice and they may interact with the ways in which women relate to themselves and to criminal justice institutions in such a way as to allow for a different way of doing justice. In this chapter, I discuss the agencies and their practices so as to provide a picture of alternative justice as a site of governance. In the following chapters, I examine the precise subjects and mentalities of governance that are produced and mobilized in the work that these agencies do.

I also use governmentality to understand the larger context of governance within which these agencies operate: neoliberalism. Neoliberalism is a political rationality that has been much used and debated. It has become, in some cases, a simple answer to a wide variety of complex sociological questions. Often, when we pose "why?" questions, "neoliberalism" is offered as the short and easy answer. Here I use neoliberalism not to answer a why question but to help situate my "how" questions: How is alternative justice practised? How are women governed in alternative justice? How does this relate to the criminal justice system? While on its own neoliberalism is an inadequate answer, we cannot understand the complexity of our contemporary moment without engaging with it. In order to do so, here I offer a brief outline of the ways in which scholars have used governmentality to understand neoliberalism and how this assists the study of alternative justice.

Neoliberalism, understood from a governmentality perspective, is not simply an economic, or even political, project; rather, it is a mode of governance. Neoliberalism is a way of thinking about and acting on the conduct of citizens. Viewing neoliberalism from this perspective allows the identification of the multiple mentalities, practices, and subjectivities that are present in neoliberal governance, enabling analysts to look for the moments of failure and fracture within neoliberal projects. Larner (2000, 14) argues that, in contrast to other ways of conceptualizing neoliberalism, a governmentality approach "stresses the complexity, ambiguity and contingency of contemporary political formations to maximize possibilities for critical responses and interventions." The ability not only to see complexity but also to build the potential for critical responses is, I believe, a necessary feature of any analysis that aims to contribute to feminist research. It also holds open the potential for alternative justice to do justice differently while, at the same time, accounting for the ways in which formal justice discourse and practices affect alternative ones.

Despite emphasizing complexity and contingency, governmentality scholars argue that there are some general ways of thinking and acting that distinguish neoliberalism as a mode of governance. While these are so familiar as to seem routine, it is worth reviewing them here. These are real ways in which our ability to imagine and practice justice, both criminal and social, are constrained. One, if not the primary, distinguishing feature of neoliberalism as a governmentality is the extension of economic thinking throughout society. As populations became objects of study, "the economy" became something that we began to understand as natural and scientific. Following the "natural" rules of economic growth became a core component of good governance (Foucault 2008; Oksala 2013).

Another key aspect of neoliberalism is its framing of and interaction with citizens as individuals. Neoliberalism identifies individual causes for and solutions to what welfare liberalism would have seen as social problems. Rather than working and governing through the social or society, neoliberalism highlights the choices of individuals (Rose 1996). This fragmentation and individualization of the social makes it particularly hard for feminist and other social justice claims to be articulated and comprehended. This turning away from social obligations shifted activity from the state to families, schools, voluntary associations, and other communities. Governmentality scholars argue that, though it may seem to, neoliberalism does not involve a rolling back of the state. Rather, there is a rearticulation of governance in which individuals and communities are given active roles in governance. This comes with a responsibility, as Burchell (1996, 29) outlines: "the price for this involvement is that they must assume active responsibility for these activities, both for carrying them out and, of course, for their outcomes, and in doing so they are required to conduct themselves in accordance with the appropriate (or approved) model of action." The choices open to individuals then are not infinite; instead, they are highly circumscribed, with many modes of action rendered unintelligible in neoliberal terms.

Individuals, and the communities to which they belong, are responsibilized to govern themselves *appropriately*. This responsibilization is an ongoing process whereby "the subject must first be shaped, guided and moulded into one capable of responsibility" (Dean 1999, 165). This ability to mobilize individuals and to induce them, without direct intervention, to act in a way that is consistent with the aims of governing authorities is termed "government at a distance," and it is a hallmark of neoliberal governance (Garland 1997; Rose 1996; Rose and Miller 1992).

These characteristics of neoliberal governance have been analyzed in the governance of crime. Garland (1996, 452) identifies government at a distance through a responsibilization strategy that involves "the central government seeking to act upon crime not in a direct fashion through state agencies (police, courts, prisons, social work, etc.) but instead by acting indirectly, seeking to activate action on the part of non-state agencies and organizations." Potential victims are responsible for preventing their victimization, and they, along with their community, are held responsible for crime. Stanko (1995) provides an early account of the ways in which government responds to women's fear of crime by encouraging them to take steps to avoid the riskiness of certain public spaces. Community centres, business owners, families, and individuals are also exhorted to do their part to prevent crime (Crawford 1997). Neoliberalism is a highly problematic from of governance when it comes to thinking about crime, criminalized women, and social justice. As Pollack and Rossiter (2010, 156) argue, "the ascendency of neoliberal ideology effectively derails local and international advocacy, such as gender- and race-based claims for justice," by removing the state as the entity to which social justice demands can be made and by focusing on individual responsibility.

Woolford and Ratner (2008, 32) use governmentality to think about alternative justice, and they construct the concept of the informal-formal justice complex – "the cultural, economic and political relations within the juridical field through which adversarial/punitive and conciliatory/restorative justice forms coexist and reinforce one another, despite their apparent competition." This complex can only be understood when placed within the broader social and political context of neoliberalism. The concept of neoliberalism puts limits on the optimistic calls for community alternatives by recognizing the ways informal justice practices are bound to, dependent upon, and constitutive of formal practices. The informal-formal justice complex is also useful in that it acknowledges the overlap of the two types of justice without necessarily finding that the latter dominates the former. We can recognize the influence of formal system discourse and practices on the informal and still "approach the question of whether or not these informal elements or 'moments' hold any potential as a space from which can be launched an internal critique that challenges the ways in which current legal practices tend to reflect the interests of dominant social actors" (Woolford and Ratner 2008, 4). The agencies under study here, made up as they are of informal and formal elements, are situated within this justice complex.

Offering "Alternative" Justice in the Informal-Formal Complex

The variety of work engaged in by staff and the agencies differentiates them from the criminal justice system. The provision of support, the activist work, and the strong grounding of many of the agencies and staff in Indigenous culture all offer criminalized women something different than does the justice system. It is the presence of the justice work, even that which could be considered informal, that prevents the programs the agencies offer from being wholly "alternative" to the formal system. Their educational and reintegrative work mirrors some of what is offered in the justice system. Of course, the supervisory work of staff is justice system work.

Despite the presence of formal justice system elements, the participants identified a variety of features that they felt distinguished their work from that of the criminal justice system. Most of the agencies' programs insist on a flexible process. The types of workshops prescribed for participants, their interactions with victims, the type of programming offered, all of these things can and should vary from case to case. As Mike noted, "I mean it might look different for every client." Andi emphasized: "We really have to be flexible in what our approach is going to be, you know? Yeah, I think the key word is we have to be flexible." Flexibility is built into the agencies' approach to account for two main factors: (1) the type of offence (for some agencies different offences will trigger different workshops or programming), and (2) the individual's circumstances. Participants from different agencies explained this feature of their programs:

> So, we try to support them however it is we can. Either by maybe giving them a homework package or coming out to their house on a home visit. We try to schedule things so it's easier for them, provide bus tickets, those sorts of thing. So, we try to set out realistic, attainable goals for them. (Andrea)
>
> We also look at what the client's strengths, interests and goals are and incorporate those gifts. (Ariel)
>
> Yeah, I think for me the biggest difference is that it's, this is individual, like here it isn't a prescribed "this is how this case is going to go because this is how all these types of cases go." It's personal, so we want to talk to these particular people about their particular experience and build both the process and the outcome from that. (Erika)

In the last quote, Erika contrasts her program's flexibility to what is found in the formal system, where consistency and treating everyone the same are foundational principles. Staff saw their flexibility as a key reason for their success. As Andi noted, they strive "to help women find a way that fits them, you know. There's no magic solution of what's going to work for each woman. That just doesn't exist. So yeah, it's really finding what works for each woman."

Staff also emphasized the relational nature of their agencies and approaches. For the Onashowewin and Mediation Services, both of whom work from an explicitly restorative justice perspective, relationship building is a stated objective. Onashowewin's website proclaims: "The objective of Onashowewin is to help restore, heal and transform relationships and the community." Part of Onashowewin's mandate is "to work to repair damaged relationships between victim and offender." Similarly, Mediation Services promises that, "in all our work – community and court-referred mediations and our training programs – we promote and use the principle of participation to help restore and build positive relationships." This relationship is central for both agencies: both offer victim-offender mediation and see the healing, transforming, or building of this relationship as key to what they do.

For those agencies that do not work with victims, relationship building remains a priority, although the relationship they speak about shifts and is primarily between staff and the women they serve. Establishing and building this relationship is a pivotal part of all the agencies' programs. As Kate stated, "so much of the job is about relationship building." Julie explained that "the key thing first with any individual is developing a relationship." Participants described relationship in a variety of ways, from "a working relationship" (Kate), to a "connection" (Mike, Kirsten, Erika), to a "role model" (Julie), to an "auntie" (Emily), or even a "mother" (Kate).

The reasons for building a strong relationship with the women they serve varied among participants. For some it was an end in itself, a way to humanize the process. The staff get to know the women and

> some of them [the women] just come by to get some shampoo and feminine hygiene products but it's still, "Hey, why don't we have a cup of coffee. How's it going? What have you been up to?" I think that matters as opposed to being a number, you know. Sitting in the remand with nothing to do and, you know, I get women who call me sometimes from the remand. There's nothing [there] right? (Sarah)

Agencies and staff spoke about the importance of giving criminalized women "a chance to speak and be heard" (program document). One participant said, "for me it's giving people a voice" (Kirsten). In order to do this there must be a relationship. There is a connection between staff and participants, while "there isn't that connection with the court program or with the court system" (Kirsten). Mike also highlighted this difference between the court system and the agencies' programming:

> Well when you go to court I think the obvious difference is the disconnect. Is, there you have the judge, you have the Crown, you have the lawyer. You have the youth here. The court speaks, the lawyer speaks, the judge speaks, and then they say, "Okay dude that's what's going to happen." And the kids are like, "Alright." That's it. "See you next court date." When they come here they have opportunities to speak about, you know, their life. Their relationships.

For some participants, relationship building is a necessary part of assisting women. As Mike noted: "You can't help somebody if you can't connect with them. If they don't want to talk to you then you're not going to get very far." Some participants needed to build a relationship in order to fulfill other parts of their job, such as information collection. As Julie described it:

> So, women will come in and we will go through our intake, which is broken up into different sections of someone's life ... Usually

that takes time. Just to get through that process because the key thing first with any individual is developing a relationship. So, if you just sit with somebody you don't know and ask them all these personal questions – you have to get a sense from them.

In other cases, it was felt that a relationship was necessary for counselling purposes: "A lot of people don't expect to sit here and cry their hearts out but that's what happens because all of a sudden somebody's listening and really hearing what happened to them. They feel safe in order to be able to let that go" (Andrea). For others, building a relationship was a step towards having the women gain access to the agency's programs and community resources: "The idea is to build relationships. We don't think we're going to get them off the street necessarily but it's a way to build a relationship with them." (Sarah).

In most cases, the staff are the primary point of contact for the women and the criminal justice system. In the bail supervision program at Kihiw Iskewock Lodge, staff are justice system surrogates. They enforce legal orders and report any breaches to formal justice system authorities. In the diversionary programs, the relationship is not so close to the justice system, but staff remain in control of the women's case file. It is up to staff to report back to the court on whether or not the women's files have been successfully dealt with. Thus, the relationship between staff and criminalized women is a highly formal one. The participants, however, consistently spoke about the informal ways in which they provided support to women. They spoke about how they "provide ongoing support" (Ariel) and said that their clients sometimes "just want more support" (Kate). The Salvation Army camp describes itself as offering "support through community resources" (program document). As implied by the role identifiers of "auntie" and "mother," the relationships sometimes go beyond the scope of the program or service being offered. Women may come to the staff to ask for assistance with aspects of their lives not officially covered by the agency's program. As Emily recounted:

This morning before you came in, a woman who I know is involved in the sex trade, she missed a court date and missed a PO

> appointment. So, she wanted to see me. She was really upset. The first thing she said was "I need a hug." So, I hugged her. And then I had to say to her, "Well, you know what you need to do is to turn yourself in. The sooner, the better, there's no miracle for that." But it's always, in some ways it's, I guess, like being an auntie.

Another participant described how the women she works with lean on her for support:

> Because even on the days they don't have to report, once you build that rapport with them, if they're having problems at home or they're low on food or EIA [Employment and Income Assistance], they'll come and they'll talk and they want somebody to help them work out the crisis with them. (Kate)

While participants articulated a variety of goals for their programs, they did not make any mention of punishment or deterrence. Many of their goals were different from those that criminal justice system officials typically discuss in public, although they were similar to the principles outlined in the Task Force on Federally Sentenced Women's report, *Creating Choices*. The participants talked about healing, providing support, empowering women, teaching coping skills, advocating for the women, and teaching them to be their own advocates.

One central goal, however, echoes precisely one of the key goals of the criminal justice system. Participants from every agency spoke of their desire to reduce recidivism: "in our mind we want to reduce recidivism for Aboriginal women" (Veronica); "[a] major [success], well, for them, is not reoffending" (Kate). Agency documentation claimed the ability of several programs to reduce re-offending. The Salvation Army describes its Positive Lifestyle Program as a "tool designed to reduce recidivism," and Onashowewin states that "people entering the programs of Onashowewin are less likely to reoffend" (program document). One of the primary reasons that the criminal justice system funds community programs is to achieve lower recidivism rates; thus, it is no surprise that recidivism featured prominently throughout the interviews. One agency shared both its application for government funding and its draft agreement for funding. The agency certainly touched on recidivism in its application; however, the agreement did not set out decreased recidivism either as a service deliverable or as a performance indicator. None of the staff mentioned any data that they keep on their program's demonstrated ability to reduce recidivism. This is one example of how the ties that the agencies have to the justice system affect their work in an obvious way, but even here staff did not allow the criminal justice goal of recidivism to overtake how they framed their work. This is further complicated by the frequent references to a slightly different goal, which was to keep women out of jail:

> That's really our goal is to have people not go back to jail ... That's my whole point; I want them out of remand status. (Andi)
>
> [What is success?] Not ever going back into the justice system. (Kate)
>
> So, for me, that's what I want for them besides not going to back to jail, I want them to take whatever skills that they have and go and share it with the world. (Caitlin)
>
> So realistically our hope is that they just get stable at some point where even if they are on social assistance, don't have a job, but they're not being exploited, you know that is a huge success, or they're not going to jail anymore. (Julie)

While this goal is related to recidivism, the focus here is on the well-being of the women themselves rather than on their criminal behaviour. It is a slight difference, but it is an important one.

While many characteristics may differentiate the agencies' programs from the formal justice system, there are also a variety of features, such as the goal of reducing recidivism, that mirror that system. In most cases, the women participate in these programs because they are mandated by the formal system to do so as a condition of either having the charges against them stayed or as a condition of bail, probation, or parole. The justice system is the primary, if not the sole, point of access to these programs. The programs offered by Mediation Services, Onashowewin, and the Salvation Army qualify as new diversion because participation in them involves "screening plus programme (formal penetration is minimized by referral to programmes in the system or related to it)" (Cohen 1985, 51–52). Ariel's description of the program in which she works illustrates this: "Well, we're funded as a diversion program so that's what we have to do. If there's restitution, it must be paid. I mean there are certain things, like restitution, that we have to do to satisfy the courts but that's just the start, then we go above and beyond." The need for the criminalized woman to fulfill court requirements and program requirements is in contrast to true diversion (195), which would see the individual diverted from all justice processes. In this way, the agencies' programs are an integral part of the formal justice system's net.

We also see, in all of the agencies, not just those that offer diversionary programs, some programming that is similar to what criminalized women would undergo in the formal system – in particular, addictions and anger management programming. In many cases, the agencies and the programs they run complement the justice system by dealing with first-time offenders in ways that are similar to those employed by the justice system. They assist the court by taking on supervisory roles. They alleviate the formal justice system by relieving court dockets and prison populations. One participant identified this goal explicitly:

> The idea is that it just alleviates a lot of traffic though the court system. A lot of times, especially if they're post charge, they are being remanded, remanded, remanded. They don't necessarily have to attend every time. The Crown just looks at it and says, "Okay, they are to be completed at this date." It's kind of, not that I'd call it a fast track, but just not so much time in the court system.

Through these programs, community members – namely, staff and volunteers – take up the responsibility not only of contributing to criminalized women's rehabilitation but also of being criminal justice supervisors and processors.

The informal-formal justice complex fits with the participants' own understanding of what they do. They do not see themselves as informal; they feel connected to the formal system. Many pointed out the links between their work and the formal system, be it through funding or employment. Staff did not claim to be offering a new vision of justice or spaces free from the criminal justice system. They do, however, believe they are doing something different. They contrasted their work with that done in the formal system, and many were critical of it. They said that being separate from the formal system allowed them to perform their work, even their formal justice work, in a different way. For example, staff are able to build relationships with women even when formally supervising them.

The bail supervision program offered by Elizabeth Fry shows the overlapping nature of both informal and formal practices and relationships. The aim of the program is to get women out of remand and allow them to wait for their trial in the community. The high number of remanded prisoners is seen by some of the staff as the consequence of a racist justice system. Bail workers construct a bail plan and submit it to the court. If the court grants bail, the work the bail supervisors do with the women involves a mixture of informal supports and services, along with formal justice work. As Kate outlined:

> It's basically more one-on-one with them, helping them navigate the system. Taking them to appointments, helping them get into programs they need to, either getting on to EIA or, if they're having difficulties with EIA, advocating for them, getting them into programs like treatment, counselling, doctors' appointments. You know, we just make sure they take care of themselves. Going to court with them, right through, like, we attend court with them right throughout. Oh, and we also follow a breach protocol because we also do random curfew checks in the community, just like the police.

Here the participant focused on the informal components of her work. She added, almost as an afterthought, the formal role she plays in supervising and reporting on the women. That formal relationship enables the informal supports: without the supervisory relationship this participant would not be able to assist the women with whom she works in informal ways as they would be imprisoned. It is not the case, as described by Allspach (2010, 719), that staff "often take surveillance and control functions, rather then [sic] a helping role such as assistance in finding housing or jobs." Instead, the staff I interviewed see themselves as helping while they surveil. All of the programs contemporaneously perform informal and formal work: they are funded by the government and private fundraising efforts, and participants understand that, while their work differs from that done in the justice system, it relies on that system. These programs are clearly part of the informal-formal justice complex.

This being the case, these programs engage in "government at a distance." Garland (1997, 25) identifies community programs as key to the neoliberalization of crime control:

> Instead of removing the individual into the near-total control of a custodial confinement, these community measures seek to insert regulatory devices into the offender's natural habitat and daily routines, producing a light framework of supervision but leaving plenty of opportunity for the offender to practise self-control.

The programs discussed here play a supervisory role not only in their official capacities but also in their informal relationship building. Supervision can be strengthened through the building of relationships. Kate described a scenario in which she was forced to act in her formal capacity:

> I've had women who breach and their first question is, "Are you mad at me? You breached me, are you mad?" It's like, "No I'm not mad, I may be disappointed but let's move forward."

Here, Kate uses her informal relationship with the client to reinforce the problem with her contravening a formal legal order. As she moves through her daily routine, the client is reminded not to breach her bail conditions because it may jeopardize her relationship with Kate.

Both formal and informal justice practices provide a variety of areas in which criminalized women can make responsible choices. The programs offered by these Winnipeg agencies use neoliberal discourses and respond to women in prototypical neoliberal ways. Although they cannot be seen as total alternatives to the criminal justice system, they should not be seen as simply replicating the criminal justice system in a different site. It is not, as is sometimes argued in the transcarceral literature, that the state has completely co-opted alternative programs; rather, it is more that community programs sometimes align with the criminal justice system.

Governmentality scholars argue that a key characteristic of modern governance is how different experts and authorities are enlisted to govern at a distance. As Rose and Miller (1992, 181) argue:

> Political forces have sought to utilise, instrumentalise, and mobilize techniques and agents other than those of "the State" in order to govern "at a distance"; other authorities have sought to govern economic, familial and social arrangements according to their own programmes and to mobilize political resources for their own ends.

The agencies under study here generally offer programs that have been motivated by social justice motivations and goals: their governance program is focused on assisting criminalized women as a social group. However, they mobilize criminal justice resources to achieve this goal, both in the form of funding and by taking part in formal justice work. This move ensures that the alternative justice means of achieving goals often aligns with neoliberal means of achieving them. Rose and Miller (1992) describe the types of networks that allow government at a distance. A key aspect of these networks is that agents can translate the values of other agents into their own language and thus use them to achieve their own goals. While agents may have distinct goals and norms, they construct shared interests, and this alignment of interests facilitates governance at a distance, the primary mechanism of which is community responsibilization. Though neoliberalism works through responsibilization, the programs under consideration also have an interest in responding to criminalized women through the community. The participants are highly critical of the formal system, particularly the incarceration of women, as Andi and Caitlin describe:

> It's terrible. Yeah. It drives me crazy. Yeah, we have more women in jail on remand status. That's an embarrassment. It's horrible. You know, like, come on. It's ridiculous. Why are we filling our jails with people in remand status? It's terrible.
>
> Time stands still. For everybody. Jail guards and offenders. It just stands. It's brutal.

Staff see the community as playing a key role in protecting and providing for women:

> For me it's along the same lines, but more so in [that] I view it as the community taking care of the community. And a lot of that comes from my own spiritual background. Coming from the Native community, [it is] very much that if you've harmed the community then not only is it your job to fix it but we have to be able to help you with that because it's supporting people on, I guess, the whole continuum right down to the victim, the family, the accused, the community. (Kirsten)
>
> A lot of people want to volunteer. A lot of people want to have that direct contact, which is great. We have a lot of excellent very skilled volunteers and that's how they want to give back to the community. (Emily)

Veronica offered one of the most clearly articulated visions of how community agencies can and should be able to take up the work of the formal system and remedy some of its defects:

> There needs to be better coordination between Justice and these wonderful community agencies that are willing to work in-house and have women transition out in a natural sort of network and look at longer-term support for these women outside of jail in order to prevent recidivism ... It's laughable in a sense ... how short-sighted it is. The government – sort of – policy around provincial corrections. Because what happens is that they're in the business of keeping the same two hundred women in jail. Really. Right. So, if it's cost them $150 plus a day to keep her in a facility like that, why would you not want to have more community-run facilities that can impose restrictions and conditions if she's not a danger to society?

Here, Veronica discusses how the program can support government fiscal goals by offloading criminal justice work. Earlier in the interview, Veronica listed safety, sustainability, meeting needs, and healing as the four primary goals of the program. Although her community program takes on criminal justice responsibility, it also works to get women out of jail and prison and into the community as a necessary condition for meeting those goals.

This analysis echoes Maclean's (2013) study of micro-finance programs and the granting of small loans primarily to women in developing countries. Maclean argues that neoliberalism becomes more complex when examined in practice. Of particular relevance to my argument, she notes that "there is a potential alignment of Indigenous demands for autonomy and neoliberal policies that have reduced the state and promoted decentralization" (462). This is similar to the alignment of the interest of alternative justice staff in shrinking the role of the justice system in criminalized women's lives and the neoliberal responsibilization of the community.

We see this alignment of interest in governing through the community not only in the justice work that these agencies do but also in their social and advocacy work. Though the goals differ, the agency staff in these two areas are concerned about providing for individual criminalized women. They do not think that it *should* be the community's responsibility to provide basic necessities, but they are committed to alleviating the suffering of individual women, so they engage in social welfare provision. This, combined with the personal advocacy they engage in, leads to encouraging women to learn to be their own advocates. Staff want women to be able to address the material impacts of marginalization on their own, for their own sake and well-being, which means they end up engaging in efforts to responsibilize the individual as well as the community.

The reason "government at a distance" works through these agencies' programs is that the interests, in many cases, align with state justice objectives. While it is true that neoliberal governance means constructing responsible, educated, employed individuals, a feminist analysis also sees education and training as ways out of social marginalization. Haney (2010) found that the therapeutic community she studied framed all women's problems through a psychological lens. She argues that staff bracketed women's social marginality by *not* attending to educational and work-focused programming. It is not that the programs are doing things that are either neoliberal or social-justice oriented: often they are doing both at the same time. The reason that community program interests can be aligned with neoliberal strategies of governance is that these interests and strategies share common ground.

The formal justice system does not simply force its goals and strategies onto the informal justice system. Although some of that occurs, particularly in the ways in which the formal justice system funds and thus dictates some of the supervisory programming, there is more evidence of a subtle alignment of goals. The criminal justice system offers strategies that align well with informal goals and that allow space and latitude for programs to achieve their own goals. That space – and the fact that all of the agents in a network of governance like the justice complex bring with them their own goals, norms, and practices – means that, although dominant governance strategies are reproduced, they exist alongside other program of governance (Rose and Miller 1992). My analysis situates informal community programs within a neoliberal context so as to examine how "different formulations of neoliberalism emerge out of a multiplicity of political forces always in competition with one another, producing unintended outcomes and unexpected alignments" (Larner 2000, 16). This perspective on the ways in which community programs may both replicate and resist neoliberal goals allows us to give agency to the alternative justice participants while not over-allocating agency to neoliberal efforts as an always co-opting or over-determining force.

Looking at community-based programs through the lens of governmentality allows us to locate them in this complex as strategies of governance. The fact that these programs are offered by non-profit organizations and community agencies does not nullify the authority they have over criminalized women. Nor does it nullify the differences between them and the formal justice system. Governing authorities bring their own objectives, values, and strategies to the task of governance. We can examine the agencies and the programs they run as having a meaningful role in governing criminalized women without equating them with the criminal justice system. This allows us to see how they may both replicate formal justice system goals and strategies as well as challenge them. Critical analyses of alternative justice offer some ways to think about and mitigate the dominating tendencies of seeming alternatives. Pavlich (2005, 112) draws on Jacques Derrida's work on justice to argue that identifying the ways in which justice mentalities are connected may allow us to imagine "a new horizon of justice with very different concepts and ideas." Woolford and Ratner (2008) point to potential breaks within informal justice that, with critical thought and care, may be expanded.

After examining the work in which community programs for criminalized women engage, we can no longer view such programs as complete "alternatives" to the criminal justice system. They engage in formal system work and participate in the governance of criminalized women. They create spaces that allow the justice system to divest itself of some of its own work, confident that that work will continue in the community. If we only examine the justice work conducted by alternative programs, this could lead to the conclusion that they are not providing much that differs from what is offered in the criminal justice system. The potential to practise justice differently seems weak. However, governance is never a seamless, finished project. It is something that is always pursued but never caught. As multiple authorities are brought into the process of practising "government at a distance," so is the potential for disruption and difference. Though some of their interests may align with those of the criminal justice system, these programs have a variety of practices, tools, and goals. This means that there is always the potential for resistance or, at the very least, complicating dominant logics. The fact that there are some differences between alternative justice programs and the criminal justice system suggests that there is also room to increase the potential for greater resistance. It is when we turn our attention to who these programs are governing and how participants constitute the criminalized woman that we see a key point of difference between them and the criminal justice system – one that offers room for thinking about justice and responding to criminalized women in new ways.

2

Alternative Subjects: Construction of the Criminalized Woman by Alternate Program Staff

> So as far as alternatives to justice, I mean this is part of the reason why we have this program because we found, I mean, people would make these decisions. Are they horrible criminals? No. They're not. They're your mother, your aunt, your sister, your best friend, right? So, they have a lot of embarrassment and shame and so they can't share that with anybody.
>
> (Sarah)

> The women we work with in this province, over 84 percent of the women are Aboriginal and they're poor, and usually the other 16 percent of the women, if they're not racialized, usually poverty is an issue as well.
>
> (Emily)

> Then it's up to the individual to go do it because we're all women, we're all adults. It's teaching initiative as well, right, and responsibility and structure.
>
> (Caitlin)

THE ALTERNATIVE JUSTICE programs studied here are firmly situated within the informal/formal justice complex and can be analyzed as examples of government at a distance, making them spaces in which dominant discourses and practices are reproduced. A close examination of the ways in which the programs construct the subject of governance – the criminalized woman – however, shows that these spaces are also spaces of resistance.

One of the tasks of a governmentality analysis is to trace the ways that particular governable subjects are constituted within strategies of governance. For Foucault, there is no stable subject that exists prior to the exercise of power. This means that the subject cannot be thought of as the *originator* of power but, rather, as the *effect* of power. This is not to say that the subject is fully determined and passive in its being constituted through neoliberal governmentality. The subject is constituted not simply by one disciplinary discourse but by many, and "subjectivity, like power, discourse and discipline, needs to be understood as multivalent and complexly constructed" (McLaren 2002, 60). So, while subjects may be constituted as docile or neoliberal, they are at the same time produced as sexual, able, and with agency. Butler (1995, 46) argues that "to claim the subject is constituted is not to claim that it is determined." Allen (2011) uses the concept of autonomy rather than agency to get at the capacity for subjects to act in a way that is not wholly determined by power. She argues that, while the "conditions of possibility for subjectivity" are discursively constructed through power relations, the subject must take those conditions up. The subject is continually reconstituted, and, in this process, she participates in her reconstitution. As a part of this process, Allen argues, we can see the autonomy of the subject, in the sense that subjects have the capacity to reflect on the power relations that constitute their subjectivity and can work on the self with practices of self-transformation.[1] Although the subject is an effect of power she is also its vehicle (Foucault 1980).

Feminist criminologists have taken these Foucauldian ideas to examine the ways in which women are discursively brought into law and justice as subjects. Smart (1992) traces the ways in which the "bad mother" is brought into being through law, arguing that this mother works to create the boundaries around "normal" and "good" mothering practices. McCorkel (2013, 12) traces the gendered and racialized ways that medical discourses on addiction and neoliberal discourses on responsibility in prison construct a "self that must be 'surrendered' to a lifelong process of external management and control." Hannah-Moffat (2001) adds social reformer and feminist knowledge claims to those that affect how the criminal justice system constitutes and responds to criminalized women. These studies have added detail and depth to Martin's (1988, 14) Foucauldian feminist claim:

> Woman, as a category of meaning, and women have been subject to the gaze, the interventions, and the control of medical, psychoanalytic, and aesthetic experts who do the work of limiting and regulating what it means to be a woman in line with the exigencies of their own discursive fields and legitimating truths.

A Better Justice? looks at the ways in which this is done to the criminalized woman in alternative justice and, in so doing, shows that she is an effect of justice discourses, not simply their target.

This chapter begins by identifying the various ways the criminalized woman is constituted, or constructed, in dominant correctional discourse and then goes on to describe how she is constructed by alternative programs. In their analysis of how the criminalized woman is constructed in official correctional discourse, feminists have identified three main subjectivities: the neoliberal subject, the psychologized woman, and the victimized woman. There are a number of co-existing subjectivities present in the alterative justice discourse as well, as neither the criminal justice system nor the alternative programs imagine the criminalized woman in a singular way. The subjectivities constituted by staff and agencies in the community echo but do not simply duplicate the criminal justice system. In fact, they differ in one primary way: the overriding subject they construct is one that holds great potential for acknowledging difference and offering an alternative subject position for criminalized women. It is here, in the ways that the programs and staff think about the women with whom they work, that we see the opening of new spaces of thought.

The Criminalized Woman in Correctional Discourses

The criminalized woman appears in correctional discourse in a variety of ways. In keeping with the general mode of governance identified by criminologists, the criminalized woman in criminal justice discourse is often a neoliberal subject (Shantz, Kilty, Frigon 2009; Snider 2014; Hannah-Moffat 2001). The neoliberal subject of corrections is, or should be after correctional intervention, a prudent, self-interested subject (Garland 1997). This subject must take responsibility for her actions, both past and future. She is responsibilized through such self-governing strategies as empowerment (Hannah-Moffat 2000). Correctional understandings of empowerment focus on the subject's ability to analyze her past behaviour and make good choices in the future. An empowered criminalized woman "is responsible for her own self-governance and for the minimization and management of her needs and of her risk to the public or herself" (Hannah-Moffat 2000, 32). Risk assessments, and risk logic, are crucial tools used to construct this subject. Risk logic, in correctional discourse, involves identifying criminogenic "needs," defined as variables that are linked at the population level to recidivism and that can be changed (Hannah-Moffat 2004). Women are assessed in order to identify needs such as employment, substance abuse, and attitude. These assessments were originally designed with men in mind and have been used, with little adaptation, to assess women (Hannah-Moffat and Shaw 2001; Maurutto and Hannah-Moffat 2006). Once a woman's "needs" have been identified and interpreted as important because, and only because, they correspond to risk, it is then up to the woman to manage those criminogenic needs. This responsibilization is accomplished through the woman's correctional plan, through programming such as anger management and addictions treatment, and through parole and probation conditions (Turnbull and Hannah-Moffat 2009). Although the neoliberal subject is common in correctional discourse, it does not exist alone: two other primary subjects exist alongside it.

The criminalized woman is often constructed as the psychologized woman. Here, her offending behaviour is pathologized and the response to her is treatment (Kilty 2012; Maidment 2006b; Pollack 2000). Both historically and in contemporary justice discourse we see a reliance on psychological constructs to make sense of women's criminal behaviour. The use of gender-specific disorders as criminal defences, such as battered woman syndrome or postpartum depression, takes women's behaviour, including their criminal behaviour, as indicative of individual pathology and attributes it to psychological disorders (Comack and Brickey 2007). The primary response to this woman in the Canadian correctional context is to medicate her and provide some cognitive behavioural programming (Kilty 2012).[2]

This construction serves to differentiate the criminalized woman from the criminalized man and from other women. A psychological construction of women is often contrasted with a construction of men as rational offenders (McCorkel 2003). Female offenders are often seen as deviating from both legal and gender norms, as "administrators, staff and decision makers use psychological rather than structural explanations to account for women's criminality and justify this by reporting, in great detail, inmates' departures from appropriate gender displays" (69). Overall this approach reifies the criminalized woman's "criminal" status and constructs her as clearly different from the non-criminalized woman (Comack and Brickey 2007; Maidment 2006a, 2006b).

The criminalized woman is generally constructed by feminist criminologists and advocates as the victimized woman or the woman in trouble (Comack 1996; Snider 2003, 2014). This woman commits crime because of social oppression. She generally does not pose a risk to the community; instead, the community poses a risk to her. The woman in trouble commits crime as a result of the violence that has been done to her (Comack 1996; Pollack 2000). This victimized woman, while constituted in scholarship and advocacy, has been taken up in correctional discourse, though with some alterations. The Task Force on Federally Sentenced Women and the report it produced, *Creating Choices*, presents a feminist understanding of the criminalized woman, noting that "representatives of women's groups and others who share their beliefs, stress that such issues as poverty, racism, wife battering and sexual abuse are centrally linked to women's crime" (TFFSW 1990, 68). This understanding is exemplified in the preface to the report: "By reducing inequities which limit choice, by preventing violence which breeds violence, our long-term goal will reduce the pain which contributes to behaviour which harms others" (2). Despite being grounded in feminist research and theory, this conceptualization was embraced by the Correctional Service of Canada and is used in the construction of the risky/at risk female subject (Hannah-Moffat 2001).

The dominant construction of the criminalized woman in contemporary Canadian correctional discourses is an amalgamation of the woman in trouble and the psychologized woman, and it incorporates neoliberal ideas around risk. She is, as Hannah-Moffat (2005, 31) identifies her, the "transformative risk subject" who is "amenable to targeted therapeutic interventions." In contrast to the static risk subject, this woman has criminogenic needs that are intervenable (e.g., employment, substance abuse, and attitude), and, when addressed, it is expected that her risk of recidivism will be lowered. The subject has the gender specificity of the woman in trouble and the psychologized woman, but that gender-informed perspective has been absorbed into risk logic (Hannah-Moffat 2004). This woman is constructed by first translating her gender-specific socio-economic oppression into gender-specific psychological deficits (Pollack 2007). Her criminal offending is a result of an inability to reason and choose appropriate courses of action or behaviour (Pollack 2006, 2007). The criminalized woman's psychological inability to make good choices is then interpreted as an integral part of her riskiness (Maidment 2006a, 2006b). The aim is to "rehabilitate" this subject, turning her into someone who can make good choices, who can become "a prudent risk/needs manager, who is responsible and able to identify risky settings, access resources, and avert situations that may result in criminal behaviour" (Hannah-Moffat 2005, 41). This discourse translates broader structural or cultural patterns of harm into individual inadequacies. Pollack (2007) uses the example of intimate partner violence to argue that this form of relational and systemic violence is viewed as affecting the psyche of the victim, which, when framed by a risk logic, puts women at greater risk of violence. For example, Hannah-Moffat (2004, 375) found, in her examination of parole decisions, that any evidence of women resisting a violent partner, particularly with defensive violence, is used "to substantiate concerns about potential future violent crime." The woman's use of violence in these instances is used to frame her as someone who generally makes bad choices rather than as someone who defended herself in the context of an ongoing abusive relationship. This is a construction that individualizes the reasons for committing crime and pulls women out of their social context, locating both the problem and the solution within the individual (Hannah-Moffat 2010; Maidment 2006a, 2006b; Pollack 2000).

Recalling the concept of the informal/formal justice complex, it should come as no surprise that these same subject positions have been found in alternative programs. Woolford and Ratner (2008) show how informal programs are imbued with and reproduce formal justice rationalities. Similarly, feminist scholars have begun to analyze community-based treatment programs for criminalized women and have found that they reproduce dominant correctional logics (Haney 2010; McKim 2008). Though they have not used the justice complex concept, these authors have argued that "locating therapeutic penal treatment in the community does not guarantee that a program will meet women's needs" (McKim 2008, 321) and that we must not assume community programs are more socially just (Haney 2010). I argue that alternative justice programs in Winnipeg contain versions of dominant constructions: the criminalized woman is the neoliberal subject, the psychologized woman, and the marginalized woman. These constructions become apparent when we examine the particular ways that alternative justice program staff talk about the women with whom they work.

The Criminalized Woman in Alternative Justice Discourse

The first characteristic to note about the criminalized woman in alternative justice programs is that she is indeed a woman. Gender matters, as Emily notes, in terms of both offending behaviour and experience of the justice system: "I think due to, I would hope [we are attentive] to gender needs because certainly the pathways for women in and out of the criminal justice system is different than the pathways for men. There's also, gender needs are very different when you're in jail as a woman." Some of the community agencies work only with women. Agencies that work with both women and men make gender distinctions in terms of understanding people who offend and in terms of programming. For example, Onashowewin offers general programming for both women and men and also includes a separate women's workshop and men's workshop. Programs offered to the buyers and sellers of sex acknowledge the gendered nature of these groups. Overall, in the constructions of the criminalized woman there is a fundamental understanding that she is different from the criminalized man. The exception to this is the neoliberal subject: the focus on responsibility, choice, and individualism is gender-neutral.

The Neoliberal Subject

The criminalized woman in the formal justice system is understood to be a neoliberal subject – a rational individual who has made the (bad) choice to commit crime. This understanding is present in alternative justice programs as well. The criminalized woman can make a variety of choices in her life, all of which are pertinent to her offending behaviour. Staff discussed a wide range of choices available to criminalized women, and, in most cases, they framed those choices in terms of women making the wrong ones. For example, the choice to be in better (i.e., nonviolent) relationships: "Being stuck in relationships they don't know how to get out of. Not knowing how to choose relationships" (Andrea). The ability to commit to changing her life is seen as something that is freely chosen, as is evident in how Caitlin identifies the struggles women face: "Themselves. I think a big thing is that self-defeated attitude. You know, not wanting to try." The fact that she has committed a crime demonstrates a woman's inability to make the right choices. Throughout the data it seems that her criminal behaviour is the result not of an innate deficiency, disease, or social oppression; rather, it is the result of bad decision making:

> They learned what they're doing by, you know, just the way of life that they are in. And they don't know that there is another way of life, they don't know how to step out of it in order to make those changes and in order to make their life better. (Andrea)

The solution for the neoliberal subject is simple: she must learn to make good choices. The ability to choose (correctly) is understood to be a learned ability. She has learned to make bad choices due to familial and other relationships. This means that the neoliberal subject can also learn to make better choices, something the programs are supposed to be able to help her do. Andi described her work as assisting women in making the good choices they need to make in order to live a good life.

> How to get education. How to complete the education. How to have a stable life. How to find new routines. Not going, you know, ... [to] dial a drug dealer. Be the person that's in training so they can have a legal way to have an income ... You know, don't go back [to jail]. Please. It's a better life. I really help them to form new habits. How to make good choices. So we're very involved. Yeah, we're very involved ... It's a better life. I really help them to form new habits. How to make good choices."

Mike described the idea behind one of Onashowewin's workshops: "basically we all have, like, a choice in life, and we have one life to live and, you know, do it right, kind of thing." The desire to change, as well as the idea that committing crime is undesirable and unnecessary, is inherent in the discussion of change: "because everybody wants to change their life, right?" (Kate).

In order to make better choices, to change her life, this version of the criminalized woman must first take responsibility for her actions. This is a key neoliberal idea, and it was present throughout the interviews. Criminalized women must take full responsibility for their criminality in order to be eligible to participate in several of the community-based programs, particularly the diversionary ones. Mike explained this requirement, which is the same for all of the diversion programs: "If they come in and they're like, 'Yeah I was there but didn't do it' or 'Someone else did it,' if they're not accepting responsibility for their part, for what they've been charged with, then we send it back." For programs that work with women on bail or post-conviction, there are different official assumptions; for example, those on bail still retain the presumption of innocence and so staff are careful not to talk about their responsibility for the crime. Both bail workers, in fact, emphasized that the women with whom they work have not been found guilty:

> And remember, they're innocent until proven guilty so I'm not going to be like, "Oh, you did this." That's not my job, that's for a judge, not my job. I want nothing to do with that. That's not my place. No, you're innocent until, that's the reality.
>
> We talk to the lawyer, not about [the details of] the charge, because we don't need to know, we just need to know what they've been charged with because they're innocent until proven guilty, and even if they are guilty we still, Elizabeth Fry Society, still helps them.

Both bail supervisors also spoke broadly about how they try to cultivate women's responsibility:

> I make them deal with a lot of their shit. Yeah, so I make them deal with their crap. Because if you don't, how are you going

> to move forward? How is that going to happen? It's pretty intense.
>
> So the woman can show [to the courts] that she's done a lot of work on herself. Because you see a lot of growth. I tell them, it doesn't happen overnight, it takes time. So, each little thing, it's just baby steps.

This work is done while the women are on bail, and it is work that staff encourage despite noting that the women have no legal recognition of responsibility at the bail stage of proceedings.

Staff at Kihiw Iskewock Lodge work with women who have already been convicted and found legally responsible, so no further acknowledgment of responsibility for their crime is required. Although there is no formal rule about taking responsibility, there is often a strong sense among staff that there is a need to do so. We see this emphasis on responsibility in Caitlin's words:

> She's fully aware, you know, so you have some women who take full responsibility of their actions and then the ones that are like, "Well, that's not my fault it's just wrong time, wrong person wrong time." No, there's no accidents, you know what I mean. That's something they really have to realize. You put yourself in that position, you need to accept responsibility, move along.

Even when the participants did not speak directly about responsibility, it was evident in their discussions of choice and change: if we choose to act we must take responsibility for those actions.

The neoliberal subject must take responsibility for her previous bad choices and for moving forward in a good, legal way. This emphasis may be found in Andrea's definition of success and in Onashowewin's description of one of its workshops, in which every client must participate:

> Someone who learns to take responsibility for the wrong, the harm, that they have caused. To put it behind them and go

> forward in a good direction. Somebody who can understand that and make better choices for themselves. (Andrea)
>
> The main focus is making positive and healthy decisions and life choices. Participants discuss the negative impacts of the poor choices that have led to criminal offence, and participants are encouraged to assume responsibility for their actions. (Onashowewin)

The precise choice that the women made, in terms of the particular crime they committed, is generally absent from my data. The criminalized woman, as a neoliberal subject, did not simply commit a criminal act: instead, she is understood to have lived a criminal lifestyle. Sarah explains: "Some, you know, their lifestyle is very, dysfunctional, for a lack of better word." Andi talks about the need to keep women busy to deflect them from their criminal lifestyle: "If they're not out doing it on their own, because we know if they're just sitting around doing nothing then eventually they'll drift back into their, for a lack of a better word, criminalized lifestyle." Julie compares the lifestyle found in the sex trade to a foreign culture:

> The whole world around them, they're not really aware of, kind of, the blinders are on and they just kind of see where they're at. It's very hard for people to see, kind of, what mainstream society is doing. Right? And depending on how long they've been in the sex trade culture, that's, it's such a way of life. How can I describe it for you that's not going to take five hours? Okay, when someone comes from a different culture, right, maybe they're coming from the Sudan. Right. Coming into Canada. Culture shock, right? Completely different and their values and beliefs and the norms and the rules and the economics and the politics. The whole culture of those communities and then coming here to Canada. Different rules, different laws, different beliefs, different religion. It's just a whole culture shock, right? So, people who have been in the sex trade a long time, again, that's their culture and there's rules in the sex trade. Their values and beliefs are different.

The criminogenic lifestyle is understood, as is the ability to choose a pro-social life, to be the result of social learning. The criminalized woman has learned not only from the men with whom she has had intimate relationships but also from her family and the different communities with which she is affiliated. As Andrea explained: "They learned what they're doing by, you know, just the way of life that they are in. And they don't know that there is another way of life." Choosing not to associate with those from whom they have learned this lifestyle becomes one more choice the women must make, though Andi notes that it is not an easy one: "There's a lot of hurdles and then there's the hurdle of staying away from the people who will bring you back into the life." The solution is to, in Julie's words, "re-socialize" the criminalized woman so that she will become a law-abiding member of the "mainstream" community.

The idea of crime as a lifestyle reinforces the ideas of choice and responsibility. All of the aspects of a lifestyle – attitude, beliefs, values, and behaviour – can be changed if the individual wants to change them. In almost every interview and document that refers to crime as a lifestyle there is a corresponding reference to the individual's ability to change this lifestyle. For instance, a program document from Kihiw Iskewock Lodge stresses the Lodge's goal "to provide them [criminalized women] with resources, opportunities and support to successfully change their lifestyles to the point where they will become pro-social members of the community." At two different points in our interview, Andi stressed: "How to have a stable life. How to find new routines ... I really help them to form new habits. How to make good choices." The idea of a lifestyle, though not discussed in the formal criminal justice discourse, is a neoliberal one. The belief that we are all free, autonomous consumers who can pick up and put down any lifestyle we choose is a dominant neoliberal idea. Rose (1999, 86) details how decisions that used to be based on tradition, obligation, social status, or a sense of what is natural are increasingly seen as "practices of freedom" and as "lifestyle decisions made by autonomous individuals seeking to fulfill themselves and gain personal happiness."

Constructing a woman's offending as a lifestyle choice accomplishes two conflicting things. First and most obvious, situating her offending as a lifestyle decision rather than as a survival tactic or the manifestation of illness functions to construct the criminalized woman as a neoliberal subject. However, Rose argues that the ideas of lifestyle and choice are not typically available to marginalized groups like criminalized women. He contends that marginalized groups are "excluded from the regime of choice" (89) and are responded to with a mix of strategies that include more punitive techniques of governance. Following from this, the second function of understanding her offending as a lifestyle choice, and indeed as an outcome of the constitution of the criminalized woman as a neoliberal subject, is to normalize her. This is an interesting break from the many ways in which criminalized women have been imagined historically as the unredeemable "other" or "monster" (Faith 1993). Snider (2003, 367) argues that many of the ways that policy discourse has constituted the female offender, "the predatory, rational, calculating Female Criminal, the violent gang girl or the irresponsible, out-of-control Bad Mother/Child Abuser," have justified the increased use of incarceration. The neoliberal subject, in her normalization, is a "regular" person who has made a poor lifestyle choice and may actually be harder to incarcerate. This is not enough to rehabilitate this subject as a feminist position. It may be worth considering how normalizing the criminalized woman may (or may not) be useful in furthering feminist claims.

The criminalized woman is also constituted as a neoliberal subject via her individualization. Much of what I have already talked about contains the tacit assumption that we are discussing the problems and abilities of an individual. Her ability to choose, her choice of a criminal lifestyle, and the responsibility she must take for that lifestyle all speak to an individualized understanding of the criminalized woman. The problem of her criminal behaviour is in her individual bad choices; the solution to her criminal behaviour is in her learning to make better ones. Participants also emphasized individual responsibility. Mike talked about individual choice in this way: "So I think its personal choice too. What do you want to do? Take responsibility for yourself." Caitlin talked about taking on a teaching role, stressing to women that, "in order for you to appreciate things a little bit more you have to do it for yourself." She observed that "one of their biggest challenges is overcoming themselves and stepping outside of their boxes." When asked to identify the main difference between her program and the formal justice system Caitlin responded, "You can't work on yourself when you're in jail." Here there is an assumption that it is the individual who needs to change rather than the social conditions that structure her life.

In contrast to the dominant risk logic of the formal criminal justice system, my data contain virtually no mention of the "riskiness" of the criminalized woman. Veronica acknowledged that women come in with a risk index but then quickly switched her focus to their safety: "We know they're at risk and we know there's all kinds of stuff, right? But safety is very different. Safety is her own personal safety: A. [And then] safety of the people around her: B." Similarly, none of my participants use the language of criminogenic needs. They did not adopt the risk/need language that permeates discussions of the criminalized woman in the formal system. Despite this absence, when staff described the programs they offer, it was often clear that there is an inherent assumption that the target of these programs is the neoliberal subject. However, when asked to describe the women with whom they work, the subject that the staff constructs looks very different.

The Psychologized Woman

Alongside the neoliberal subject is the psychologized woman. Though none of the staff with whom I spoke have a clinical background, and none of the programs specifically identify clinical goals or even hint at a clinical philosophy, the data reveal that the criminalized woman is clearly psychologized. Although HIV and physical disabilities were briefly mentioned, the primary focus was mental health: the criminalized woman often suffers from poor mental health.

The participants spoke to the psychological health of criminalized women in a number of different ways. There is the to-be-expected understanding of the psychological causes of criminal behaviour. Participants sometimes framed the women's offending in terms of pain, shame, or anger. Consider Andrea's comments:

> And that would help them to look at the other underlying issues that happen, which is possibly causing them to get into conflict with the law. Okay. A lot of it comes from pain, shame, anger, poverty, and we discuss all of those things in individual meetings and that helps them.

Staff encourage the women to self-assess: "What are your triggers? This, that, and the other thing, and work through the whole process" (Caitlin). They discussed depression and anxiety. Veronica described the complexity of the women's mental health needs: "So when you combine high anxiety, anti-anxiety drugs, high dependence, low sustainability and lots of behavioural modification. So, forget it. This is what we're seeing." One participant in particular understood certain women's offending as rooted in the physiological and psychological experience of menopause. As Erika noted, "Mental health issues can be a huge challenge and often contribute to offending, and the system doesn't have really good capacity for dealing with those." Similarly, Andi stated, "You can't do this job without addictions and mental health." Along with recognizing that the criminal justice system is ill equipped to deal with mental health issues, participants spoke to their difficulty in providing programs to women with mental health concerns. Specifically, attention deficit hyperactivity disorder and foetal alcohol spectrum disorder were frequently mentioned as being challenges in terms of working with women (and men) in the programs.

In these programs, the psychologized woman is understood to have addiction issues. Sarah and Caitlin said that the vast majority of the women with whom they deal are addicted to a substance. Specific substances are not identified, but several interviews and documents mention the role of addiction in the lives of criminalized women.

> How do you survive addictions? So, these are like, I would say the majority are addicted ... We were looking at what are the key factors: addictions and housing. These are two of the main things that we really need [to] address. (Sarah)
>
> My history is addictions and mental health the first half of my career, and you can't do this job without dealing with addictions and mental health. (Andi)
>
> For the adult women, in particular, do they need child care, again housing, [checking] where their addictions are at. (Julie)

Participants see addiction as a cause of crime, and frequent mention is made of "crimes of addiction and poverty" (Veronica). Staff often contrasted these types of offences with violent crimes. Addiction is also referred to as a symptom of victimization, echoing the themes of the feminist victimization-criminalization continuum. In one specific reference, a program document states that addictions "reflect the symptoms of abuse and neglect." Much of the data on women involved in the sex trade speak to the pervasiveness of addiction, and Sarah talked about the inevitability of continuing addictions: "You know, is she going back on the street? Probably. Is she going back for another hit? Probably. Next time you see her she may be strung out on crack." The pervasiveness of this link between criminalized women and addictions can be seen in Veronica's observation that criminalized women either suffer from addictions or have been told that they suffer from them. One program's standardized intake form includes questions about treatment, and, overall, many participants treat addiction as unremarkable. This speaks to an overriding "common sense" interpretation of the criminalized woman as struggling with addiction. Participants were not asked about addictions, and they routinely mentioned them in an offhand way when discussing other issues. No matter the type of programming or the stage of criminal justice processing (diversion, bail, or post-release from jail or prison), staff seemed to assume that addiction was a core part of the criminalized woman's life.

Another component of the psychologized woman is her experience of trauma, which is linked to a variety of causes: violence, life situation, the family, and sexual abuse. Staff also link trauma to a number of consequences: violence, case complexity, limited life skills, disability, and being triggered. Trauma was sometimes understood to be the cause of women's offending behaviour, although it was more commonly discussed as a factor that must be accounted for when designing programming. The ways in which the staff discussed trauma were typically gendered: they strongly linked the women's trauma to sexual abuse and other forms of gendered violence.

Trauma, above and beyond the mainstream understanding of it, is also understood as having a uniquely Indigenous meaning. Participants discussed the loss of family and community connections as traumatizing for Indigenous women, men, and children. Mike described the impact of separating children from their families as incomprehensible:

> You have this kid who was taken away from their family. Just from that very act alone, it's just so unnatural. It just affects a human in such a profound way. I can't even comprehend it. I myself was apprehended at a very young age so I understand how it is. I'm still trying to understand how much that affected me.

Several participants spoke of the need to heal from the harm caused by residential schools and other practices of colonization. Andrea commented:

> The taking of the land and the displacement, you know, residential schools, the Sixties Scoop. We need to go back far enough so we can truly see ourselves and then come forward and know who we are and then take our individual lives and what has happened to us so we can heal that part.

Trauma was described as being particularly rampant among Indigenous women. Staff attributed this to the high levels of violence in Indigenous women's lives. This understanding of the violence faced by Indigenous women in Canada is borne out in the large-scale victimization study conducted by Statistics Canada. The most recent Victimization Survey recorded a sexual assault rate of 115 incidents per 1,000 population for Indigenous women, compared to a rate of 35 per 1,000 for non-Indigenous women (Perreault 2015). While Indigenous women make up only 2 percent of the Canadian population, they make up 16 percent of women who are murdered or who go missing (RCMP 2014). Staff stressed that this violence is not only a problem for individual women but that it is also an intergenerational, family, and community issue.

Although staff draw on psy-discourses in their constitution of this subject, there is very little identification of specific psychological disorders, and the agencies offer very little cognitive-behavioural programming. There is, in fact, some critique of that programming. Kilty (2012, 178) identifies a number of problems with the way this medicalized discourse manifests in the coercive prescription of psychotropic medications in prisons, including "the use of medication as a technology of social control (including both prescription and denial of medication), women's lack of the right to refuse medications, and a lack of access to nonmedical therapeutic intervention." While the programs continue to provide medications for women, participants criticized the over-medication of women: "They heavily medicate them in prison. Let them out and good luck getting a prescription. Good luck seeing a doctor. So, women often relapse very early, as soon as they get out" (Veronica).

The psychologized woman is, in a manner similar to the neoliberal subject, an individual. The cause of her offending behaviour is located within her, at the individual level. She is not, however, responsibilized in the same way as is the neoliberal subject. The psychologized woman is seen to be suffering from an illness or an injury. The injury, whatever form it takes, is seen as central while the crime is seen as peripheral, perhaps even as a symptom of the injury. If the woman's injury is healed the criminal behaviour will end. Responsibility still figures here, but it is not responsibility for past actions; rather, the psychologized woman must take responsibility for her healing going forward.

The programs under study here, no matter the degree to which they medicalized the criminalized woman, are not treatment programs. Elizabeth Fry and Onashowewin offered in-house workshops on understanding and dealing with addiction. The other agencies referred women out to treatment programs and were cognizant of the unique challenges they face in such programming. Thus, the discourse created by staff contained some of the understandings of the psychologized woman that have been noted in the literature. However, because they do not offer actual treatment, they avoided many of the therapeutic strategies and tools that feminist scholars have found problematic for criminalized women, particularly behavioural modification, peer surveillance, and total erasure of social structure (Beck 2006). The staff did not reduce the women to their illness or their addiction, and this stands in stark contrast to what is revealed in research such as McCorkel's (2013) ethnography of an in-prison drug treatment program. McCorkel documents the ways in which the staff of that program focus on breaking down the women's sense of self in order to rebuild it in a process of habilitation. She says that one of the major problems of the program "was that it reduced their self-identities to one or two disreputable categories and denied them their complexity and their respectability" (225). Staff at the alternative justice programs identified the psychologized woman in ways that strove to acknowledge that complexity, as can be seen even more clearly in the final subjectivity constituted by these programs: the marginalized woman.

The Marginalized Woman

Finally, and importantly, the data also contain a criminalized woman subject who is similar to Comack's (1996) woman in trouble – the marginalized woman. She exists in the margins of society, and this location shapes her criminal behaviour. This woman reflects feminist understandings of marginalization and criminalization. A common critique of feminist discourse is that the concept of woman, and the type of oppression a woman suffers, is understood to be homogenous, most often inherently premised on white, middle-class standards.[3] This was not the case in the data; in fact, Emily specifically spoke to the problems with this way of understanding women:

> In terms of gender, we try and run the agency based on an Aboriginal paradigm where everyone is involved in the circle. We do not use a Western liberal feminist ideology because Western liberal feminism, which, basically not unless they declare otherwise, all other women's agencies are based upon, subsumes race and social economic class.

The criminalized woman is understood by participants to be oppressed by a variety of social structures in complex ways. She is an Indigenous woman; she is poor; she is marginalized through her gender and, particularly, her role as a mother; she is uneducated; and she is the victim of violence. This is a wholly intersectional framing of her marginalization as all of these oppressions rely on and lead to one another.

The construction of this woman begins with identifying her as an Indigenous woman, as Kate does: "Mostly, I would say, in the five years I would say 90 percent were Aboriginal." This type of statement is made throughout the interviews across the different agencies. The criminalized woman in the data is often, if not always, an Indigenous woman. While participants generally refer to the women with whom they work as Aboriginal or Indigenous, a few, such as Emily, point to more specific identities: "And it would appear and she [agency's spiritual care worker] concurred with this, the majority are First Nations. So, when we say 'Aboriginal' there's not a lot of Métis women. There's a couple of Inuit but not very many. So, [the] majority are First Nations." Along with recognizing this identity, staff acknowledged the multiple structural oppressions faced by the Indigenous woman. She is not simply Indigenous, facing racism and racist structures, surviving residential schools; she is an Indigenous woman, she is also typically poor. For these programs, dealing with criminalized women and, in particular, those who do not have the financial resources to deal with their criminalization, there is an overriding logic that the criminalized woman is Indigenous.

This identity was not simply noticed by participants; instead, independent of any questions on my part about race or social structure, the colonial experience and structures were discussed again and again. Colonization is seen as having a tremendous impact on the lives of the women and their families. Staff explained that colonization has caused intergenerational trauma, violence, and dysfunction in families, which has led to shame and to a disruption in the building of Indigenous identity. Mike identifies the many harms perpetrated by residential schools and connects that colonial institution to contemporary harms:

> The underlying issues stem from residential schools. Justice Sinclair has said it will take seven generations for young people to overcome residential school syndrome. We're still seeing it continue right at the ground level. The effects of what happened a long time ago, it affects them. They don't know their language, they don't know why they're in dysfunctional places, it's normal for them, it's a continuing cycle.

Dysfunctional families and communities were then identified as a source of criminal behaviour, lifestyle, and choices. Participants also spoke to the lack of informal supports for women when they do get into trouble. They do not have someone they can call because their intimate relationships are dysfunctional or because their family members are in prison as well. As Emily explained: "Most of the women, particularly the Aboriginal women, come from fragmented families. So, there isn't even a nuclear family let alone the structure of the extended family to provide a safety net. So that's something that we try to do."

Participants also spoke to their experience dealing with a racist criminal justice system. Chris pointed to the Aboriginal Justice Inquiry (AJI),[4] which looked broadly into the relationship between the criminal justice system and Aboriginal people. A number of recommendations were included in its final report, and Chris voiced his frustration with their implementation:

> Manitoba is so far behind in implementing the AJI recommendations. Correctional Service of Canada just issued a report about overrepresentation and how they're going to start implementing the recommendations. It's been twenty years, kind of late. The answers are there, the recommendations are there. More and more Aboriginal people are going to be going to jail with these new justice bills.

Two participants were particularly critical of Gladue reports:[5]

> Probation services have been, and still are, attaching a risk assessment form to the Gladue Report. Which goes against the entire point of the Gladue. This all hinders a fair trial, and fair outcomes. It hinders the outcomes and plans used if they [are] found guilty when at sentencing there's a risk assessment that goes against that person. What we need are independent Gladues. Reports that don't have a risk assessment, just life history and recommendations for changing the lifestyle. The impact of these reports can be great, we're talking years versus months inside or even no jail time.
>
> There's Gladue, they're trying but, you see, in Manitoba, you have to remember, if they had Gladue courts, all the courts would have to be Gladue except a couple. So that means that you'd have to have Aboriginal judges, Aboriginal lawyers, Aboriginal court workers. Is Robson Hall [a law school] increasing the amount of law students to accommodate a Gladue system? No. So, this is about, you know, white privilege.

Mike spoke about the hostile relationship between police and Indigenous people. Emily put it most bluntly: "The other thing, of course, is that justice here is racialized. That's about racism."

The marginalized woman is also typically a mother, yet she is understood to be a mother who does not have custody of her children and/or who was in Child and Family Services care herself. This was not considered to be the result of her own bad choices as an Indigenous mother; instead, social structure was repeatedly discussed. Residential schools, the Sixties Scoop, and contemporary child welfare services came up time and time again, although I asked no specific questions about them. There is a recognition that, although the marginalized woman has lost her children, this was due to structural racism rather than to her personal failing as an individual mother. Apprehension is understood as happening because of her Indigenous status rather than because of her criminalized woman status. While there are certainly incidents in which children need to be removed from the home for safety reasons, Blackstock et al.'s (2004, 912) research on child welfare in Canada found that "cases of substantiated or suspected maltreatment involving Aboriginal children were more likely to involve neglect and, in particular, supervision issues, rather than physical or sexual abuse." The authors of that research point to poverty, housing issues, and addiction – a complex result of colonization – as the primary factors influencing the removal of children. This research echoes Veronica's suspicions that children are not always removed because of violence or harm:

> They, to the detriment of children and families, rip them apart for the best interest of somebody, not really sure, children, foster parents? That's not always demonstrated, what the safety or protection issues are when children are apprehended. There are some that need to be. I think it's inconsistent. I think they spend a ton of money in that system that they don't need to.

The marginalized woman's childhood is also understood to have been marked by apprehension. Kate highlighted this aspect of women's history:

> Because they didn't get the parenting, because the Scoop, the Sixties Scoops and children being placed into foster care, house to house to house. Because I've heard stories of some kids, when they were children, being taken from, being placed in forty to sixty homes in their lives, and to me that's horrific. That's just not right. Not right.

Participants discussed the intergenerational nature of CFS involvement and family dysfunction, and the ways that it is linked to colonization and the oppression of Indigenous people in Canada. Veronica told a story of one resident in order to illustrate intergenerational impacts.

> I think of this one mom, grandma actually. She's really the Don of this family, honestly. Her daughter-in-law, her kids, have all resided [in jail]. So, this is a woman, to give you an example. Most of her kids were in care ... Her conflict with the law revolved around drugs and poverty, trafficking. Is waiting to be sentenced for like the last three years or so. So three of her daughters are deceased and all in a very short period of time. She has one grandchild she's cared for, one who she's fighting with CFS for. Her, you know, she has another baby that's just come into the picture through one of her other kids. The mother is her daughter, resides in the same facility, who basically was in youth corrections since she was a kid for double homicide. This is the complexity and the nature of what we're dealing with.

The marginalized woman is also poor. She is not a member of the working class or the working poor; rather, she is constructed as the poorest of the poor. She is either receiving social assistance or living on the street. This emerged in the data as a strong commonsense logic, revealed both through the frequency with which participants spoke of her poverty and through the offhanded way in which they mentioned it. For example, one of the bail supervisors at Elizabeth Fry described the process of working with a woman at the beginning of the program. If the bail hearing is successful, after putting together a bail report, the next step is meeting the woman's very basic needs:

> I mean what's basic needs? They've already got the housing part set up because the thing is the judge isn't going to release the person unless they have a house, or a place to live, so that's already taken care of. So, if they're living here or in the community, are they on assistance? Because you need money to pay bills and food. So, I will get an emergency kit at Winnipeg Harvest, the day they're released, so at least they have something to start with.

Poverty was often brought up in response to seemingly unrelated questions, such as: "Can you describe the work your program does?" Participants spoke about how they are dealing with crimes of poverty, how they look to underlying issues such as poverty, how the women they deal with are "probably on EIA [Employment and Income Assistance]" (Veronica). Many of the staff understood poverty to be a causal factor in the women's offending behaviour. As Andi put it: "Poverty will breed unhealthy ways to feed your family at times." It is also seen as influencing the marginalized woman's interactions with the criminal justice system. For some women it may mean the difference between being in jail and being in the community. As a bail supervisor at Elizabeth Fry explained:

> She may have been granted bail but I can't pick her up. Yeah. So, then she sits and waits for a bed. That's lousy, you know. Like she knows she's got bail. The bail hearing happened and the judge said, "Yes you have bail," but there's no bed available. There's nowhere in the community this woman can live because she can't afford to.

The challenges listed by the participants also speak to the extreme nature of the poverty experienced by the criminalized woman. The participants constructed the criminalized woman as needing assistance with a variety of basic needs: shelter, food, identification, and transportation.

When asked "What are the biggest challenges facing the women you work with?," we would expect a neoliberal discourse to centre on the woman's own motivation and choice-making, her inability to conduct herself properly, and her lack of taking responsibility. There was some mention of this in the data. Caitlin identified the biggest challenge as: "Themselves. I think a big thing is that self-defeating attitude. You know, not wanting to try." A psychologized construction would primarily reference addiction, medication, getting a proper diagnosis, and treatment options, which was a minor theme in the data. The most commonly identified challenge was the most basic of needs: housing.

> Well, especially when they get through camp, and they are ready to make changes but there's nowhere for them to go ... Housing is a huge challenge. Especially if they have children residing with them. (Sarah)
>
> So, the biggest challenge is housing. Addictions, well the addictions part. But housing right now is a major thing and that's on the basic needs and it's hard to get housing. (Kate)
>
> Housing. Housing would be the hardest. It's, as you know, we have a very low vacancy rate. The average rent here in the city of a one bedroom is at least $750. Single women on welfare, rent is $270 or something. (Julie)

Participants consistently discussed the need for housing, and while this appears to clearly contribute to a marginalized subject position, the critical literature documents the various ways in which poverty (particularly the need for housing) is framed within neoliberalism. The neoliberal themes discussed earlier, the responsibilization, empowerment, and decontextualization of individuals from the social structure, operate within services for homeless individuals (see, for example, Ranasinghe 2017; Woolford and Curran 2011; Whiteford 2010) and are taken up by those individuals (see, for example, Dej, 2016; Woolford and Nelund 2013). Dej

(2016, 131), in her observations and interviews with shelter users, finds that these neoliberal themes interact with psy-discourses to create a context in which "those who reject the reductionist model by contextualizing their homeless and distressed status within social, cultural, political, economic, and historical factors are negatively judged by their homeless peers for making excuses and failing to take ownership over their lives."

Staff in this study do not engage in this type of judgment or in the framing of this need as a cause of crime. Housing needs are not translated into a risk factor: there is simply the recognition that the woman needs a place to live. She is not blamed for her inability to find a place to live. There is no mention of how her criminal record, or bad choices, or lack of responsibility have contributed to her homelessness. Instead, the focus is on the inadequacy of EIA and the general lack of affordable housing in the city: "I think for housing from EIA for one person is $200 and I think it's $280. Which, what are you going to get? It's not good. So, it's really hard to find affordable housing for the women" (Kate). It is not because she is a criminal that she cannot find housing: it is because she is poor. Again, this is an intersectional understanding. The criminalized woman is not simply a poor person: she is a poor, Indigenous mother.

Participants also worked to break down the binary of offender versus victim. This is a classic feminist argument pertaining to women offenders: that they are both victims and offenders (Comack 2006). Participants spoke to this directly: "I would have to say victim offender, offender victim, probably both" (Veronica). They also spoke to it indirectly by referring to the criminalized woman's vulnerability, about how "[she is] vulnerable to exploitation by drug dealers and pimps" (Julie); to "the personal prisons that they live within on a daily basis" (program document); "to go[ing] back to dysfunctional communities, families, partners, and back into this sort of cycle. Maybe knowing more but none the less they're certainly vulnerable" (Veronica). Women are seen as particularly vulnerable to violence and to death. Sarah speaks about the value of just being able to check in with women:

> We're happy to see you. Come on in, kind of thing. Because we've lost women. That's the reality of those that we work with. Tomorrow they may not be here. And not because [of] anything that would be normal, right? Whether it's overdosing or it's some form of violence. Who knows?

The violence that the women face and the trauma that they have sustained were also highlighted. Women are victimized by intimate partners, dysfunctional families, and structural arrangements. This is particularly true with regard to a woman's identity as an Indigenous woman. There was reference to her becoming missing or murdered, the systemic violence she faces, the intergenerational trauma, and the overall amount of violence in her life.

Though this recognition of victimization was a strong component of the data, I hesitate to use the label of the victimized woman or the woman in trouble. The participants focused less on a woman's victimization and more on her marginalization. The woman in trouble is understood to commit crime because of her victimization (Comack and Brickey 2007). That construction makes a more direct link between her violent victimization and her offending than did the participants. It also locates her victimization in the interpersonal violence of spousal or family abuse, while participants more frequently spoke to her structural victimization. As with the other conceptualizations of the criminalized woman, here, too, her specific criminal acts were rarely spoken of; instead, the focus of the discussion was on her life and her overall position and placement within overlapping social structures.

Co-Existing Subjectivities

Throughout the interviews and the program documents, the criminalized woman is constituted as a neoliberal subject, a psychologized woman, and a marginalized woman. These identities co-exist. It is not the case that some participants construct her in one way while others construct her in another way: the different constructions occur at the same time. For instance, Sarah identified the criminalized woman's chosen lifestyle, and thus her responsibility for having lost her kids, but she also medicalizes her through reference to addiction and recognizes her social situation (i.e., her poverty):

> How do you lose your children, because of your lifestyle or whatever, how do you get out of bed in the morning? How do you survive addictions? So, these are, like, I would say the majority are addicted. So, you're living in poverty, you're uneducated for the most part, and you're addicted.

More commonly, at one point in the interview the criminalized woman may look one way while at another point she may look a different way. This presentation must be complicated further. It is not simply that these identities can be neatly separated; rather, each subjectivity modifies and changes the others.

The risky neoliberal subject is undermined by both the psychologized and marginalized woman. Her ability to choose both to commit crime and to change her life, an ability fundamental to the neoliberal construction, is partially nullified by her other subject positions. The psychologized woman has very little agency. If her criminal behaviour is a result of an addiction or mental illness then she cannot possibly be said to choose that behaviour. Addiction is seen as something requiring treatment, as something that stems from abuse and trauma, not simply as a bad choice. Though the marginalized woman may have more agency than the psychologized woman, it is similarly constrained. Chris spoke about residential schools and how "we're still seeing it continue right at the ground level. The effects of what happened a long time ago, it affects them." Social structure also constrains her choices regarding moving forward. As one program explained: "The agency residents are women who, victimized either in their interpersonal relationships or through systemic neglect, are left without resources to independently make the life changes they feel are necessary." Throughout the data the criminalized woman is constructed as a passive rather than as an active participant in her offending behaviour. Participants spoke of her as someone who is "vulnerable" (Veronica; Julie), "floundering" (Caitlin), and "victimized" (Kirsten). The criminalized woman was often "lured back" or would "fall back into traps" (Veronica), and thus she "ended up being charged" (Andrea). Her criminal circumstance and life history were described as "tragedy" (Andi). Her crimes are not the well thought out actions of the rational individual; rather, they are "crimes of poverty and addiction" (Veronica).

The individualized nature of the neoliberal subject is also undermined by both the relational and structural foci of the marginalized woman. Participants mentioned two main types of relationships: intimate partners and families. Women are "in an abusive relationship" (Sarah) and "it's their partner who gets them into the situations" (Andrea), or "it's maybe from past relationships, being beaten down" (Caitlin). Oftentimes "you're born in to a gang" (Andi), and "sometimes family is the problem" (Emily). The participants spoke about how criminalized women have "experienced a lifetime of family dysfunction" (Veronica). The common sense assumption running throughout the data was that the criminalized woman does not have a healthy family and that she is in abusive relationships. One exceptional case that one participant discussed stressed how close the woman was to her mother and how supportive the latter was. That this is presented as an exceptional case reinforces the idea that the norm for criminalized women is to have weak parental and familial relationships.

The aim of program facilitators is to strengthen or build relationships. In her study of a community treatment program, McKim (2008, 310) found that "the staff aimed to make Belinda an unencumbered, self-managing individual through focusing on herself. They did not invoke Belinda's responsibility to her son but viewed her desire to engage in active mothering as evidence of her disorder rather than a sign of responsibility." In contrast, in looking at my data one gets the sense that the criminalized woman's role as mother is encouraged. Much of the time participants talked about assisting the women to get their children back. Caring for children was seen as a way of reducing recidivism, and regaining custody was seen as a motivator for getting one's life together: "We find that if we can help women reconnect with their families and children, that's what leads to success for them" (Julie). Motherhood, the ability to parent, was described as a skill or ability that can be learned and should be taught. Overall, participants were very supportive of the women mothering their own children, even when it was acknowledged that they may have to learn how to do so. CFS was identified as a cause of many problems, one of which was that "past involvement with child welfare tends to translate into current and future involvement" (program document). Many of the women involved in these programs have contact with CFS. Veronica noted that "most are CFS-involved," and staff discussed the fact that CFS is a difficult bureaucracy to manage once children have been apprehended. According to Veronica:

> We had a real rough ride with CFS. They dumped the kids off because the foster home placement broke down. This woman had never parented her kids. She's been in jail most of their life. Dumped the kids off. We came up with safety plans. Okay, let's start reunification, she's been clean for over a year now. Then because the foster parents squawked they turned around and took the kids. And then put a bursary on her baby. So, we fought tooth and nail to have not one more child go into the system with attachment disorder because they took her away when they were a baby. So, we won that one. So, she's going to be raising her little baby. Under the supervision order, which we're totally fine with as long as she can care for her child.

Families are emotionally affected by the removal of their members. Participants also discussed CFS in the broader context of the removal of Indigenous children from their communities and the resulting loss of culture and identity.

> It starts when a kid is apprehended, say from the time they're two years old from the time they're a teenager, and they're in a different home and they're not with their own people. They're

> not in their own culture and they're not in their own community. There is going to be racism in there. There is going to be some sense of a longing that's missing. There's going to be questions that can't be answered, that they know nothing about, but they should but they're not taught because nobody else knows them in the community so they become almost lost. (Mike)

Staff also spoke about the importance of their own relationship to the women with whom they worked. In contrast to Beck's (2006) finding that staff did not want to take care of the women, instead wanting the women to take care of themselves, participants often spoke of their role in helping and caring for their clients. According to Kate:

> I'm just going to say sometimes you have to play mother with the women. The women, and this may be deviating from your question, I've had some women wanting me to adopt them. And I say, "I can't because number one you're an adult, number two you're a client and it's a conflict." But because you build that relationship there are a few that call me "mom," but the thing is some of, sometimes you have to talk to them as a mother because they may not have gotten that, not by their fault, and I think that goes back to the colonization of the Aboriginal people.

Relationships, particularly parental ones, family ones, and also whole community ones, are seen as important, in contrast to individualizing neoliberal strategies.

Even when participants individualized the criminalized woman, they placed her within a structural context. As Julie stated:

> Really trying to get folks to be able to have that own self-determination in their lives, right? And how they make those decisions and that they have the right to make those decisions and make choices and that they have the right to information.

> They have the right to education. They have the right to, you know, social justices. Just ensure that they know all those things. Because most women who have been impoverished, or exploited, or oppressed usually don't have that information, right? The information can be power in a lot of situations so.

Although this participant begins by talking about choice and individuals, she moves to placing that choice within structural constraints, acknowledging that social structure affects an individual's ability to know and choose.

The psychologized woman is, through her construction as ill or injured, necessarily pathologized. However, throughout the data this is tempered by an absence of the most obvious way of pathologizing her – references to specific mental disorders. Although anxiety and depression are mentioned, there is no mention of more specific psychological disorders, no mention of official diagnoses. Participants avoid these diagnostic descriptions in an attempt to normalize the woman: she is rarely labelled an offender. Pollack (2006, 247) argues:

> The label of "offender" operates within a criminal justice and correctional script and relies upon an Othering process that separates offenders (those Other women) from those writing about and working with them. Not only does this dualism stigmatize and create artificial boundaries and hierarchies, but it also reifies women's identity as permanently criminal or offending.

This tendency was resisted by participants, who consistently spoke to the various ways in which the criminalized woman was the same as them (and other women). Rather than Othering the criminalized woman, several staff very clearly stated that anyone could become criminalized. Kate argued: "They're experiencing the same things as other people. Except, again, the charges. And society frowns upon people who have been charged. But anyone could be charged. Anybody could, people break the law, what is it, like, five times a day." Likewise, Caitlin observed: "When you think about it three-quarters probably, actually the entire population could have ended up in jail at one point, just some of us weren't caught and some of us were. We're just people, like everybody else. So what if you have a background, everybody has a background." Andi offered a similar sentiment as part of her motivation for doing this work: "I just, I don't know, I've seen so many people in my life where they could have gone down that path. They could have gone down because of really hard times and tragic moments, and some of us have just been given the right people at the right time in our lives so that it didn't end up here."

Many of the participants challenged my framing of the issues faced by criminalized women and pointed out that housing and addiction are challenges for all women. Sarah, for one, said:

> I think just women overall, period. Right? Whether they're in conflict with the law or not. If you're looking at someone who's living in poverty, single mom, whatever, these are the challenges. Housing, education, employment. Sometimes its addictions, sometimes it's not, parental skills. All these different types of things. So, I mean, overall it's a challenge for a lot of women, period.

This narrative works against medicalizing and pathologizing criminalized women and instead situates them in relation to the social context women face more broadly. While recognizing the issues with which criminalized women must deal in relation to their criminalized status, participants were adamant that these women have much in common with non-criminalized marginalized women. The criminalized woman's identity as a woman or single mom or Indigenous person is constructed as a more pertinent identity than is her identity as a criminalized person.

Although the psychologized woman is individualized, the root of her psychological problems is consistently located in her marginalization. This is in direct contrast to the psychologized woman's presence in official justice discourse, where mental illness "diagnoses depoliticize and fail to adequately account for the socio-political, cultural and thus structural basis for the distress women experience" (Kilty 2012, 165). Here the psychologized woman's psychological issues are consistently placed within their structural context. Throughout their discussions of trauma, participants tended to resist a solely individual, psychological understanding of trauma. Instead, to a large extent, staff used a sociological framing of trauma, one that Comack (2018) argues is necessary when making sense of criminalized women's lives. Comack is highly critical of the individualized understandings of trauma that are typically found in criminological literature and, instead, argues for a framing in which "trauma is understood not as a psychological disorder or disease but as the lived experience of residing in a settler-colonial, capitalist, patriarchal society" (28). Although Mike spoke of the Indigenous criminalized woman as "wired a little differently," he suggests that this is directly linked to colonization:

> The First Nations population is wired differently from the time they were young and going back from residential schools to being taken away. When you get taken away as a kid your wiring gets shifted around and you're going to be different. You get disconnected. You have a society that wants nothing to do with you.

Again and again, the Indigenous criminalized woman's trauma was seen as the result of intergenerational trauma caused by colonization:

> So, what we're dealing with is – and some are direct survivors of residential school because the last residential school closed in 1996, so women who are younger than me have gone to residential schools that are in their thirties. So, some are direct survivors and then it's the next generation. So their needs are about healing. And there just isn't enough services. I mean, healing [is] not just in terms of therapy to deal with traumas but

> healing is also about – they've missed out, as you can cite earlier about what I said, even coping with conflict. That's about healing. (Emily)

Social oppression was identified as a source of psychological distress, as were the criminal justice responses to the criminalized woman. Prison was identified as a source of anxiety and depression: "And they have a lot of anxiety, particularly in young women who have been institutionalized for long periods of time. You can see it. You can see their level of dependence is quite high" (Veronica). Prison is seen as the problematic factor, as something that induces trauma and anxiety and leads to the over-medication of women. Though the criminalized woman is understood through a medical framework, that framework is then looked at through the larger lens of marginalization. In many ways, participants translated the personal troubles of women into the political problems of society.

The marginalized woman is affected by the psychologized woman and the neoliberal subject. If, throughout the data, the personal was made political, the reverse is also true. The structural context was translated into psychological problems, the result of which was poor individual choices. This translation process has been repeatedly identified in the literature pertaining to the formal justice system (Hannah-Moffat 2005; Kilty 2012; Pollack 2007). It takes place here as well through the presence of the neoliberal subject and the psychologized woman. The simple fact that these subjectivities co-exist with the marginalized woman individualizes the criminalized woman. My data also contain direct examples of the transformation of structural problems into personal ones. One program describes its clients' backgrounds as follows:

> Many Aboriginal women who experienced incarceration are survivors of childhood sexual abuse, trauma and family violence. Many of them have had child welfare, justice and/or other system involvement and interventions at a very young age in their lives, resulting in being totally disconnected from

> positive family supports and/or extended family supports in their communities. Due to having experienced systemic and/or familial neglect and abuse, many Aboriginal women who have experienced incarceration also have a negative sense of self and identity. (Program document)

This excerpt begins by recognizing the victimization of criminalized women and placing it in the context of social system involvement and oppression; however, it ends by discussing the impact of this involvement on women's individual sense of self and identity. This process is not identical to the one that has been identified in correctional discourse and practice. As Pollack (2007, 160) argues:

> When incorporated into correction logics and discourses, the victimization narrative becomes psychologized; that is, there tends to be a focus on the psychological and emotional impact of such experiences and how impaired thinking, decision making, and lack of emotional control lead women to commit crimes. The psyche of the criminalized women is the site at which reformation occurs.

The victimization narrative that Pollack speaks of was not present in my data; instead, there was a broader marginalization discourse. This being the case, it is not the criminalized woman's psyche that becomes the primary focus of reform, it is her life as a whole, particularly her education and skills.

As participants described the women with whom they work and the work they do, three distinct subjectivities became evident. In their discussions with me, and in the program documents I analyzed, the programs constituted the criminalized woman as the neoliberal subject, the psychologized woman, and the marginalized woman. These three identities affect each other. Sometimes a translation of the marginalized woman's social oppression into personal defects was apparent, as it is in much of the literature. But the reverse was also true. The recognition of social structure and disadvantage in the marginalized woman's material experiences nullifies the responsibility and ability to choose that is demanded of the neoliberal subject. Though these subjectivities co-exist and influence one another, the predominant subjectivity that participants used to construct the criminalized woman was the marginalized woman.

Here we see the criminalized woman being constructed through a social justice lens. This is contrary to much of the literature that has examined community programs. This type of understanding can help create the breaks in the informal/formal justice complex that Woolford and Ratner (2008) identify. The marginalized woman is a figure that challenges dominant constructions of criminalized women. Rather than reproduce neoliberal and criminal justice ideas of responsibility and self-governance, the programs construct the criminalized woman in a way that links her personal needs and actions to social structural oppression, and this affects the work that the programs do. It leads them to engage not only in criminal justice work but also in social work (broadly understood), culture work, and advocacy work. This more contextual understanding of the criminalized woman means that it is not simply her criminal offending that is the object of governance or advocacy; rather, it is her whole life. This subject, the marginalized woman, is the starting point for how staff think and respond to criminalized women.

3

Alternative Mentalities: Framing Alternative Justice through Neoliberal and Ethic of Care Mentalities

> This workshop is mandatory for all clients to attend. The main focus is making positive and healthy decisions and life choices. Participants discuss the negative impacts of the poor choices that have led to criminal offence and participants are encouraged to assume responsibility for their actions.
>
> (Onashowewin)

> It's always just to be kind and respectful and honest with people and keep to your word. Right. You say you're going to do something, do it. So just [a] basic humanitarian type approach, right? That's what the feedback from the women coming here is that they feel safe here. They don't feel judged here. You know, so that's why we are, we always have people coming for years to our program. They keep coming back. To touch base or they need a little support somewhere.
>
> (Julie)

A KEY TASK for those using a governmentality framework, along with identifying the subject of governance, is to trace and think through the mentalities or rationalities of governance. Constituting the criminalized woman in these varied ways necessitates that the staff think about their work differently. This chapter traces two governing mentalities that shape and organize the work of the agencies and staff – the neoliberal mentality and the ethic of care mentality. These mentalities reflect a tension between neoliberal and social justice approaches to criminalized women. When we examine the programs' justice practices, a strong neoliberal mentality of governance is clear as the formal justice practices and the informal personal development programs aim to rework the criminalized woman into a responsible neoliberal subject. This chapter begins by showing the presence of this mentality. The alternative mentality, an ethic of care, is also present in the programs and can be seen when the focus is on the social, advocacy, and culture work performed by staff.

Neoliberal Mentality

The justice work that is performed by the agencies, including in the programs that involve formal supervision as well as in the informal personal development programs, shows an approach to working with criminalized women that is grounded in neoliberal ideas. As discussed in the previous chapter, neoliberal governance involves the constitution of a new political subjectivity. Rose (1996, 57) argues that this involves a new subject of government, one who can and should "maximize their quality of life through acts of choice, according their life a meaning and value to the extent that it can be rationalized as the outcome of choices made or choices to be made." This rationality constructs the individual as "a rational, free, responsible, and prudent consumer who is capable of minimizing and managing risk" (Hannah-Moffat 2001, 164). Governing techniques focus on techniques of self-formation to encourage the construction of that individual subjectivity. The aim is to construct active subjects who make their own choices within the bounds drawn by governmental power. Those boundaries are aligned with the interests of governing authorities. Garland (1997, 191) points to the types of choices that are out of bounds when discussing prisoners: "The prisoner who enjoys criminal behaviour, or who embraces the consequences of crime, or for whom a law-abiding life is not a viable option, will be deemed 'irresponsible,' no matter how self-aware and autonomous his or her actions are." Individuals are expected to actively manage their lives and make good choices, including not committing crime (Rose 2000).

Many of the programs offered by the agencies, particularly the informal and formal justice programs, are directed at constructing a self-governing subject. A key characteristic of neoliberalism is the enactment of governance through engaging individuals in an "array of programmes for their ethical reconstruction as active citizens" (Rose 1996, 60). We see this in the variety of programs offered by the agencies, particularly those aimed at education, training, and personal development. The theme that runs through all of these programs is the idea that knowing yourself will allow you to change yourself. The objective is to instill in individuals the ability to reflexively understand themselves, to be self-aware and therefore to be able to act appropriately or self-govern.

Rose (1996) argues that a key aspect of the neoliberal subject is to be an expert on oneself. Individuals are expected "to adopt an educated and knowledgeable relation of self care in respect of their bodies, their minds, their forms of conduct" (59). The ability to know the self is often a stated aim of the programs or staff. For example, the Positive Lifestyle Program offered by the Salvation Army aims to enhance participants' "self awareness and coping skills." Andrea stressed that she helps her clients "know who they are and they can move forward from here." Sarah said that the work her program does involves "a lot of self-reflection," while Julie spoke about helping her clients to "find themselves again." One participant outlined a workshop she runs on relationships: "I usually start with the most important relationship, which is the relationship with themselves. They need to know and understand, be comfortable in that relationship first in order to have other relationships." Many of the programs share this participant's sense that much of the work they do is about "looking at helping individuals to examine their behaviour" (Sarah).

A key aspect of the self that can be known and acted upon is self-esteem. Self-esteem may seem like an unqualifiable good; however, feminist scholars have documented the particular use of empowerment through self-esteem as a self-governance strategy for women in a variety of contexts, including prisons (Hannah-Moffat 2001), therapeutic communities based in prison (McCorkel 2003) and the community (Haney 2010), and prostitution policy (Harrington 2012). Self-esteem becomes one more way in which we focus on improving the self and our behaviour in a manner that is shaped but not directly managed by the criminal justice system or other professionals (Cruikshank 1996). Many of the programs under study here speak to their desire to improve or build self-esteem in their clientele. The Salvation Army camp offers workshops that cover positive self-care and self-esteem. New Directions' Transition Education and Resource for Females program documents assert that its program works to "assist to stabilize living situations, promote healthy lifestyles and build confidence and self-esteem." The Native Women's Transition Centre provides "continued support to develop and enhance practical living skills that serve to build confidence and self-esteem" (program document). Onashowewin provides a workshop specifically for women that is "about building self-esteem, learning tools for making better choices, coping mechanisms" (program document). The programs offer the criminalized woman the opportunity to know herself better and to build her self-esteem.

This knowledge is then put to use in changing their behaviour. As Onashowewin proclaims on its website: "Every morning the sun rises offers the opportunity to change your life." Mike described the work his program does around anger management in this way:

> I'm trying to think about a scenario about [someone who is] passive aggressive towards you, and you can feel that energy when someone is trying to put that off. So how are you going to deal with that? We'll give A,B,C, D sort of answers. Do you do this? Do you do this? So it's kind of, we try to, like, simulate them in terms of the options that they have that's not just one way of doing things. Teach them how to explore ... different ways of dealing with anger even. When a situation gets too much ... It's just hopefully giving them some sort of tools to work that shit out.

Here program participants are taught how to recognize situations in which they may react badly. They are given appropriate options for reacting, and it is hoped that, when they leave, they will be able to make the right choices. Caitlin pointed to the importance of this type of guided self-reflection:

> They learn that the community is affected, the courts are affected, and most of all *they're* affected. They learn about those effects. A lot of the times they didn't even realize that it affected them in that way, but they're taking the time to look at how it affects them. I think that is one of the biggest, biggest lessons that they learn. Because usually people don't take time to think about themselves, they just do. And they're so busy in the world they just go on and on not realizing how things are affecting them, but like we talk about feelings and we talk about other people and we talk about the seven teachings. You know? And so, something sparks inside of them because they know it's true. And so, they stop for a minute and then they think about that. I think that really makes a difference.

Similarly, the Positive Lifestyle Program at the Salvation Army develops service users' self-awareness and coping skills "to assist them in ensuring the offence will not occur again" (program document). Here individual women are encouraged to govern themselves through their freedom, their ability to be self-aware and to make the right choices.

Throughout the data there is an underlying assumption that the individual has the ability to change, to find balance, to exercise self-determination within her current social situation. There is an assumption that the only obstacle to change is the individual herself. One participant explained to me that one of the models the programs use is the stages of change model. Originating in research on alcoholism, this model identifies different points of readiness in individuals to change their behaviour. The model has five stages: (1) the pre-contemplative stage, at which individuals do not identify a problem and so have no intention to change; (2) the contemplative stage, at which individuals are aware of the problem and are thinking about addressing it; (3) the preparation stage, at which individuals do not actively change but take significant steps towards addressing the problem; (4) the action stage, at which individuals change their behaviour; and (5) the maintenance stage, which involves sustained commitment over time to ending the problematic behaviour (Prochaska, DiClement, and Norcross 1992). Julie explained the stages of change model to me using the example of someone who is addicted to cigarettes: at first they deny there is a problem, then they acknowledge some harm, then they move from thinking about maybe buying a patch to cutting down consumption, then they move to quitting, and then they concentrate on staying away from cigarettes. She went on:

> So, it's just kind of getting them to figure things out and help guide them, right? And you can't force them through the stages, people have to figure it out for themselves and do the work for themselves. You can't do the work for them. So that's stages of change kind of, in a nutshell. We use that here with every issue that they're facing. Then, so, they come in, we do a whole intake process, we look at different parts of their lives, from justice, to housing, relationships, addictions. So, all of those different areas, we'll assess kind of where they're at because they will be in different spots.

While this model may have value when looking at addictions, it is hard to see how the women's encounters with justice, their housing needs, or their relationships could be remedied simply by their recognizing the problems and having a will to change. This assumption that the women have the ability to change lies beneath much of the education, training, and personal development programming offered by these Winnipeg agencies.

Alongside the assumption that individuals can change is the idea that individuals must do this work themselves: "So they can leave behind the jail and all that BS and start something new they've been given because they've chosen to take it" (Caitlin). Participants were sometimes adamant about this aspect of the programs, as evidenced in the above quote from Julie, who emphasizes that this work must done by the women, not the staff. Likewise, Caitlin frames women's freedom as dependent on individual choice and responsibility:

> If you're not here to work then they need to leave. Because that's the choice. You can either stay in jail or you can be let out into a place that's going to provide you with your education, your trade, your case manager needs, your counselling. Everything. Your medication. Your place to live, a roof over your head, safety or security. Or you can go to jail. Those are your choices. In terms of the sell, it depends on the individual. Like, if the individual wants to work and this is really what they want to do, then they'll do it ... They have to want to work, you don't want to work then you don't have to come here.

The programs all see themselves as assisting women, but the individual chooses to change and take advantage of the tools the programs provide. Sarah qualified her discussion of assistance to focus on women's responsibility: "In order to help people we need to help them with all of these types of things. Or give them the tools to help themselves." The programming, be it educational, training, or personal development, makes up a large part of the toolbox that the agencies provide. There is considerable evidence here for the argument that the neoliberal logic of the criminal justice system has been incorporated into alternative justice spaces (Allspach 2010). Particularly in their justice work, the criminalized woman is constituted as a neoliberal subject, and staff respond to her with neoliberal self-governance-inducing strategies.

One significant aspect of a neoliberal mentality – a strong economic rationality – is largely missing from these data. Garland (1997) identifies three features of the economic rationality, which he sees as a hallmark of contemporary responses to crime: (1) the language of economics, risk, reward, and bottom line being imported into crime control; (2) the increasing focus on objectives such as cost control, efficiency, and management; and (3) the use of fiscal practices such as budgeting and auditing extending into other types of decision making. Though the participants do give the criminalized woman the ability to choose and act rationally, they do not frame her as a client, service user, or consumer, nor did they ever discuss efficiency or cost/benefits. The ways in which staff members think about their work with criminalized women is therefore not wholly neoliberal. Indeed, much of their discourse evokes a different mentality: the ethic of care.

Ethic of Care Mentality

When the agencies' other types of work are analyzed, a very different idea and approach to the governance of criminalized women is evident. In their social and advocacy work, participants rely on an ethic of care. There is a large and diverse literature on the notion of a feminist ethic of care, beginning with Carol Gilligan's (1982) psychological work on moral development. Drawing on a variety of research projects with boys, girls, men, and women, Gilligan is critical of Kohlberg's stages of moral development. When Kohlberg's androcentric model is used to assess the moral development of girls and women, they either score at a lower stage of development than boys and men or fall entirely outside the parameters of moral response. In contrast to the abstract rights and rules that Kohlberg (see Gilligan 1982) identifies as key to moral reasoning, Gilligan argues that women speak in a "different voice" – one that emphasizes and reasons from relationships and responsibility.

More recent work on a feminist ethic of care has attempted to overcome some of the essentialist weaknesses of the original work by positing an ethic of care not as a psychological theory of the difference between men and women but as a political theory and commitment. The central work in this regard is Joan Tronto's 1993 book *Moral Boundaries: A Political Argument for an Ethic of Care.* Tronto (1993, 162) argues that an ethic of care is both a moral framework and a political idea, "that the practice of care describes the qualities necessary for democratic citizens to live together well." She contrasts care with other types of human activity, such as creativity, production, and the pursuit of pleasure, arguing that care involves starting from and considering the standpoint of others. Tronto defines care as "a species activity that includes everything that we do to maintain, continue and repair our 'world' so that we can live in it as well as possible" (103). There are four elements of care in this framework, and many of these can be clearly seen in participants' description of their work.

Tronto describes care as a practice, one that has four distinct, but related, phases: (1) caring about, (2) taking care of, (3) care-giving, and (4) care-receiving. Caring about involves recognizing that the carer needs to have the ability to take the standpoint of the one in need. In their construction of the criminalized woman, staff consistently strove to take her standpoint and to recognize a variety of her needs. Andrea spoke of trying to understand and acknowledge the particulars of each person: "And so they come here and we try to work with them in order to help them and try to do things based on their understanding or their capabilities, you know?" Erika reiterated the importance of considering the specificity of people's lives in her program's approach: "It can be a real range of things. It depends on what the participants feel is necessary." Sarah spoke about having women share their own stories as a measure of success: "But for us, the success is really just, we have a closing sharing circle, hearing their stories. If they want to share them, then you know you've made that connection." The participants' source of knowledge about criminalized women is not academic research, government reports, assessments, or files: it is the women themselves. Emily spoke about the ongoing work her agency does in this regard: "We are always looking at how we can better meet the needs of the participants."

Participants' focus on the criminalized woman's need for care, rather than the criminal justice system's needs or their own agency needs, is evident throughout the interview data. Of particular interest here is the fact that in response to my question "What is the biggest challenge the women you work with face?" almost all of the participants identified the needs the women had, and the dominant ones were those arising from the criminalized woman's social marginality. The overriding problem for the criminalized woman in my data is her marginalization. The agenda for the programs and staff becomes twofold: first, helping her cope with her marginalization by providing basic necessities and, second, helping her overcome her marginalization through training, education, and work.

Tronto's (1993) second phase of caring involves "taking care of" those recognized needs. This involves assuming responsibility for the women's care and determining how to deliver it. My follow-up question to asking about the biggest challenge the women faced was "Does your program assist with that?" In answering this question many participants displayed the second phase of care: assuming responsibility for the provision of care (i.e., taking care of). Though the needs they identified were generally beyond their scope as employees of community justice organizations, they all took responsibility for helping to meet them. Even when participants responded by saying that they were not meeting those needs, it was not a denial of responsibility but, rather, a recognition that it was too a big a job for them to accomplish alone. Sarah discussed a variety of needs that women have and some of the ways in which her program met or did not meet them. She followed up with: "Yeah. It's a lot about partnering. We also have a strategy committee that is looking at some of these gaps and challenges and where do we go from here?"

Participants presented various reasons that responsibility for care fell to them. For some it was simply because the need was present and not being addressed by anyone else: "Like, thankfully we have bus tickets funded in our program. Otherwise I don't know how this woman is going to get around" (Andi). Here the program cares for women's transportation needs because no one else does. Another participant discussed the healing work in which the program engages – not in order to meet agency needs or criminal justice needs, not because the program is obliged under law or under a formal notion of justice, but simply because the woman's need is so great:

> So, we also look at being able to work with women on a level that helps to deal with the intergenerational trauma because violence is just so prominent in Aboriginal women's lives. (Veronica)
>
> We do a lot because it's necessary. (Andi)

Several participants spoke to the potential for anyone to become a criminalized person, and, in recognizing this, they evinced an inherent sense of responsibility: they provide care to criminalized women because their positions could be reversed. For the Salvation Army, its sense of responsibility lies in its spiritual foundations:

> The Salvation Army is a church first and foremost. Because it is a church the founder wanted to reach all those people ["the prostitute, beggar, and robber" mentioned earlier in the in the interview]. How do you do that? You have to meet their physical needs and emotional needs before you can meet their spiritual needs. (Participant)

For some, the program must take responsibility because the women with whom they work lack the personal relationships that would be the usual sources of care: "Then we put that together for them [package of goods for prison] because often, like, there's no moms, sisters, and if there is a boyfriend or husband oftentimes he's not in the picture at the time of sentencing" (Emily). Andi also pointed to the lack of personal relationships: "It's my job to help them to find a routine that works for them that they can enforce in their life so they feel that comfort. Because some of these women aren't getting that comfort from their family. Sometimes family is the problem."

These diverse notions of why staff should be providing care are encapsulated in the concept of responsibility (as practised under the ethic of care). Tronto and those who use her foundational work (e.g., Sevenhuijsen 2004; Barnes 2006) contrast responsibility with obligation. Obligation is seen as too formal and rule-bound. Tronto argues that responsibility is the better term and should be used and conceptualized broadly. Her intent is to allow for a wide range of responses and to affirm a variety of sources for the responsibility to care for each other. This flexible and open notion of responsibility is useful for validating the various reasons one may feel a responsibility to care.

Tronto's third phase of care is the activity of caregiving: meeting the need for care that people have. Tronto (1993, 107) argues that caregiving "involves physical work and almost always requires that caregivers come in contact with the objects of care." A substantial amount of the programs' activities is made up of giving care to criminalized women. Much of what participants talked about involves the provision of general assistance to the women with whom they work. All of the programs offer goods and services that are best described as care work, and staff discussed various aspects of their programs that were not directly linked to criminal justice matters, either formal or informal. With regard to the programs that are specific to criminalized women – the Prostitution Diversion Program at the Salvation Army, TERF, Kihiw Iskewock Lodge, and the various programs at Elizabeth Fry – a large portion of what they do involves meeting the women's basic needs (housing, food, material goods) and addressing their social marginalization. Onashowewin also engages in this type of work, though to a slightly lesser degree. Mediation Services, because of its focus on discrete conflicts rather than criminalized women, involves very little of this sort of work.

Several participants cited Maslow's (1943) hierarchy of needs, which organizes human need into five categories – physical, safety, belonging, esteem, and actualization – wherein the lower-level needs must be satisfied before the higher-level needs. Participants referenced Maslow's theory in a broad way, without going into too much detail or even mentioning the high-order needs of esteem and self-actualization that we might have expected given the various neoliberal self-governing strategies described above.

Instead, their focus was on the fact that if your basic needs for food, shelter, and safety are not met then it will be very difficult for you to achieve anything else.

The programs meet these needs, or at least address them, with the provision of material goods. When asked what success looks like, Sarah responded: "They're eating, eating food, you would not believe how much some of these women eat. But you know they haven't had a decent meal in however long. That to us is success." Kihiw Iskewock Lodge and Elizabeth Fry both provide housing for women. TERF and the Salvation Army both recognize the women's urgent need for housing and try to assist them in finding stable housing or in giving them a space at their Prostitution Diversion Program camp or at overnight events where they "provide vulnerable women with one night in which they are safe from the drugs and violence they face daily on the street" (program document). Beyond the basic human need for housing, the programs recognize that criminalized women need this housing to be safe and strive to provide this safety when they can. Kihiw Iskewock Lodge "provides Aboriginal women who have experienced homelessness and involvement with the criminal justice system with long-term, safe transitional housing" (program document). Veronica stressed the importance of safety: "Certainly in our program goals the first one would be safety. Safety is number one. If women aren't safe nothing else matters." Several of the programs see that women are provided with basic personal items: clothing, blankets, towels, toothbrushes, soap, menstrual hygiene products, and underwear. Many assist women with transportation by providing bus tickets. Much of what the programs do involves providing their participants with material goods.

The programs also strive to meet women's needs and provide care through non-material support. Many participants listed "support" as an aspect of their programs:

> And then they have the staff behind them helping them. You know, if I see someone who has the potential, that drive, I'm going to try that much harder to help them succeed because

> that's part of their journey. Know what I mean? I know I've had a lot of help along the way and a lot of support. (Caitlin)

Likewise, a program pamphlet emphasizes the various supports the program provides: "Support in dealing with government processes, such as obtaining personal identification, economic assistance etc. Continued support to develop and enhance practical living skills that serve to build confidence and self-esteem" (program document). Another participant stated this more bluntly: "So we try to support them however ... we can" (Andrea). They also recognized the fact that some women lack supportive people in their lives: "There isn't the informal support within your family structure so that you can get a bus ticket or to go see your PO [probation officer] so you will not be breached. So, what the women do is they will come here" (Emily). The participants discussed providing support focused on dealing with the criminal justice system but also, and predominantly, providing support in general.

The frequency with which participants mentioned general support is clear evidence for an ethic of care. To support someone is to maintain or sustain them, which fits in with Tronto's definition of care as activities that maintain, continue, and repair our world. Moreover, when they cannot meet a specific need, the programs refer the women to other agencies. This particular finding complements Welsh's (2019) work on probation and parole officers' caring behaviour, which found that, while criminalized women felt that their probation officers demonstrated caring attitudes, those officers were unable to assist with the actual provision of any material support. Welsh notes that "caring alone is insufficient for women to surmount the many institutionally constructed barriers that stand between them and rebuilding their lives" (18). This is true if staff limit their care to simple recognition of need. Participants discussed assisting women with a variety of the needs that Welsh found probation and parole officers left to the women to take care of, such as housing and child welfare advocacy.

In contrast to neoliberal risk logics, the needs we are discussing are not framed as "criminogenic needs" or risk factors, and meeting them is not framed as a way of preventing crime; rather, the provision of shelter, food, and clothing is discussed as an end in itself. This contrasts with research such as Miller's (2014, 323), in which a prison re-entry service provider "stated his program provided food, clothing, and shelter to 'take away excuses' and allow the real transformative work of prisoner reentry programming to take place." Instead, in the programs considered here, basic goods and services are provided to women because they need them in order to survive. We can see how fundamental this care work is in an example given by a participant. This participant described a case in which a pregnant young woman had shoplifted and was being processed through their alternative program.

> We talked about, like, "What's going on in your life? How is work, school, what are your plans?" She was, like, "I'm going to be at home with my mom." The mom has been a really great support, so it's no problem, it's fine. I was, like, "Okay, cool." So that's where she'll be. So it's all good. She was seven months pregnant, the following month she'd be eight months and I just thought what good are we to her at this point? What good is it going to be to set her up in workshops, bog her down with workshops and work, when she could be getting, using her time for other things like resting or just eating. I just thought to myself, there's a point where we help people and then there's a point when we can hold them back, and that was one of those instances where we're not going to help her at all.

There was nothing more to do for this woman because she did not need any care work from the program staff. Her needs were being met, and she was being supported by other people in her life.

In the above example, according to the caregiver the woman did not need any more care. Tronto's (1993) fourth stage of care is care receiving. Those who receive care respond to that care. It is important to examine this aspect of care as those who give care may misinterpret needs, and, "even if the perception of a need is correct, how the caregivers choose to meet the needs can cause new problems" (108). This is an element of the ethic of care that I cannot address directly as I did not speak to criminalized women. But my data provide the clear sense that staff feel the care they are giving is well received. Some programs, such as the Salvation Army's camp, solicit feedback from participants. Several staff from Onashowewin noted that they were getting people who came in after hearing about the agency's program from friends or family who previously used its services. Staff from other agencies talked about women coming through their programs multiple times or dropping by the agencies just to check in. This suggests not only a positive response on the part of care-receivers but also attentiveness on the part of staff. Care is both a type of work and a way to frame that work.

Co-Existing Mentalities

Present in the staff's understanding of their work are two governing mentalities: a neoliberal mentality and an ethic of care mentality. These two mentalities co-exist uneasily. They work on, and in so doing constitute, different subjects. They have different assumptions about the object and goals of governance, with one mentality reflecting dominant understandings of governance and the other doing the opposite. They do not, however, exist in isolation from each other. Much like the subjectivities in the previous chapter, these two mentalities interact in different ways. While we can see how an ethic of care mentality can align and support a neoliberal mentality, at the same time we can also see how it challenges neoliberal themes.

Aligning an Ethic of Care Mentality with a Neoliberal Mentality

One way that the two mentalities interact in my data involves the ethic of care mentality aligning with and supporting the neoliberal mentality. I examine this interaction in two main ways: (1) through a shift in the object of governance and (2) through the individualization of responsibility. Governmentality studies strive to make obvious the various mentalities governing authorities bring to governance, and one aspect of this effort is showing how authorities identify the object of governance. For example, Pavlich (2005) differentiates the object of governance in restorative justice discourse and criminal justice discourse as harm for the former and crime for the latter. Outlining restorative justice discourse, Pavlich argues: "One detects here a rationale which posits repairing or healing harm as a guiding moral vector." For the alternative justice programs studied here, neither harm nor crime is the target of intervention. Participants did not discuss the specific crimes that the women with whom they work committed. The only time criminal offences were referenced in the data was when a program was designed for specific crimes, such as the Prostitution Diversion Program. Even in these instances the crime itself is discussed more as an entry point to their agency rather than as the primary object of governance. Instead, the interviews with alternative justice staff revealed two distinct objects of governance: (1) the criminalized woman's "life" and (2) her sense of self.

The first object of governance, the criminalized woman's "life," flows from her constitution as the marginalized woman and is framed within an ethic of care. If her marginalization is the central problem, then it is also the object of governance. The goal is to change every aspect of her life, including her lifestyle, criminal offending, and addictions. For example, participants discussed helping the women to change and develop their budgeting skills: "They're allowed $50 a week that includes all their toiletries and stuff. If you think about it, $200 a month is quite a bit of money for groceries and all of their things. So, it's trying to teach them to budget. To stay within those guidelines" (Caitlin). And then there are parenting skills, along with education, employment, and recreation habits: "We really try to incorporate too within the classroom, the hardest one is the physical actually. So, getting people mobile" (Julie). This holistic focus is evident in Julie's discussion of one of the theories from which her programs work:

"Looking at the individual but within the context of the different levels, so from a macro to a micro perspective, right? Looking at the big picture issues that are going on for someone and then looking at the community and family and other systems." And her definition of success is: "if things are less harmful in their life ... just those types of steps that people have done something in their lives that makes it easier for them or safer for them." Kihiw Iskewock Lodge takes referrals from four sources, one of which is not even a criminal justice source. It will house and support women who have interactions with Child and Family Services. While the referral source distinction was made, nothing else in my conversations with Kihiw Iskewock staff suggested that women coming from a CFS referral were treated any differently than women coming from elsewhere. In the Lodge's programs and in the other agencies' programs, crime is not the primary object of governance. Instead, there is a recognition that the criminalized woman is socially marginalized, rather than simply criminal or criminalized, so the focus is on equipping her with what she needs to cope with and ultimately end her marginalization. This object of governance comes from the the criminalized woman being constituted as marginalized and is activated primarily within the participants' ethic of care discourse.

The second object of governance is the self. Here the woman's sense of self, her ability to act as an individual, is the focus. The goal of the programs is to recreate the woman's self into one that is healthy and law-abiding. The goal is to change the whole self. This point echoes and reinforces dominant criminal justice discourses that focus on the rational individual, the rational self. Feminist researchers have found this focus in a variety of criminal justice sites. McCorkel (2013, 120) points to this object of governance in her study of a drug treatment program for incarcerated women: "the source of the problem is the 'disordered' and 'unruly' self, and so this self becomes the object of control efforts." Similarly, Haney (2010) identifies this logic in a community residential facility for mothers. Carlen (2002, 235) demonstrates this focus in English criminal justice when she highlights a passage from *The*

Government's Strategy for Female Offenders: "The characteristics of women prisoners suggest that experiences such as poverty, abuse and drug addiction leads some to believe that their options are limited." The problem identified in this quote, and in the neoliberal mentality more broadly, is not the experiences of marginalization but the belief system of the woman. This is most often framed within a larger psychological discourse. The disordered self is made well, made into the rational neoliberal self, through treatment. Participants did not, to any great degree, utilize the therapeutic aspects of this discourse. When the focus shifts from how they constitute the criminalized woman to how they respond to her, the psychologized woman fades away. They acknowledge her need for medical treatment and attention (especially with regard to addiction), but they leave that response primarily to others in the form of referrals to other agencies. They do, however, discuss the need for the criminalized woman to know, work on, and ultimately change herself. When the programs focus on the neoliberal subject, using neoliberal governing mentalities, the object of governance shifts from the criminalized woman's life to her individual subjectivity, and the response is to try to make her a more responsible individual.

Though quite different in their conceptualization of the subject and in their assessments of success, the neoliberal mentality's and the ethic of care mentality's objects of governance are similar. The agencies respond to the marginalized woman by attempting to ameliorate her marginality, which involves targeting multiple aspects of her life. They do so first by meeting her basic needs and second by trying to assist her in overcoming her marginalization. Participants frequently discussed enhancing the criminalized woman's abilities and habits in order to change her life. The object of governance remains her marginalized life circumstances, and the focus is on helping the woman and facilitating her ability to change those circumstances. In order to do this, however, the programs enlist the woman herself in the project of addressing her marginalization. This can, sometimes, lead to focusing on changing the criminalized woman's sense of self in order to change her abilities and habits. In the day-to-day functioning of their programs, participants' structural analyses become individualistic. The various programs they offer no longer target the women's marginalization; instead, they target the women themselves. With the neoliberal discourse of self-governance existing alongside the programs' structural understanding of the woman's marginalization, the difference between her material life experiences and her subjectivity collapses. Structural solutions to ending marginalization and assessing life circumstances fade from view, while personal change strategies become the focus. The result is a governing strategy that ultimately reinforces the neoliberal focus on responsible self-governance.

Indeed, an ethic of care mentality is easily aligned with a neoliberal mentality through the concept of responsibility. Both mentalities articulate responsibility as a key value. Tronto (1993) argues that one of the dangers with the ethic of care is the risk of parochialism, of narrowing care to a practice in which we engage only with those close to us, thus removing the responsibility to care for those distant, unknown, or "other" to us. How, she asks, "are we to guarantee that people, who are enmeshed in their daily rounds of care-giving and care-receiving, will be able to disengage themselves from their own local concerns and to address broader needs and concerns for care?" (142). This is a tendency within the ethic of care mentality when it exists on its own. The danger that care becomes something we only give and receive in our close, personal relationships is amplified when a neoliberal mentality, stressing individual and community responsibility, is present. An ethic of care's focus on responsibility, combined with its emphasis on local and particular caregiving and receiving, sits very comfortably with a neoliberal mentality of governance. It does not challenge the idea that individuals and communities are responsible for their own well-being. Nor does it necessarily implore us to care for marginalized others. In such circumstances, an ethic of care mentality risks being added to, or co-opted by, a neoliberal mentality: individuals and communities are responsible for caring for themselves and each other.

Challenging Neoliberal Mentalities with Ethic of Care Mentalities

The ethic of care mentality can be seen as challenging neoliberal mentalities. Its presence can, in fact, rework neoliberal strategies into something different. By bringing in feminist theorizing built upon Foucault's notion of techniques of the self, we can see the potential for care discourses to change the meaning of the practices that have so far been interpreted as neoliberal. While I have thus far focused on technologies of governance used by the staff, governmentality is the contact point between governing others and governing the self. As indicated in Chapter 1, much of Foucault's work focuses on the ways in which power is mobilized in relations with others. Foucault's triangle of power focuses on the ways in which, in various relations, power is mobilized to work on individuals. Criminologists have used his ideas to analyze a diverse array of technologies of power and how they work on subjects, including in restorative justice programs (Woolford and Ratner 2008), in harm minimization drug strategies (O'Malley 1999), and in the clothing that women are permitted in prison (Bosworth 2007).

In his later works, Foucault (1994, 225, emphasis added) shifts his focus slightly, observing: "Perhaps I've insisted too much on the technology of domination and power. I am more and more interested in the interaction between oneself and others, and in the technologies of individual domination, in the mode of action that *an individual exercises upon himself*." Technologies or techniques of the self are practices "suggested or prescribed to individuals in order to determine their identity, maintain it, or transform it in terms of a certain number of ends" (87). With technologies of the self, the work one does on the self becomes central to the constitution and governance of the self as a subject. This work is relational: it is the governance of the self by the self but it is done only within and through the relations that we have with others. It is also ongoing because work on the self is never a completed project. Moreover, work on the self is bound to and uses existing discourses, practices, and relations of power.

Scholars have used a governmentality framework to conceptualize self-governing strategies, but they have generally only read those strategies as being aligned with and fulfilling a neoliberal or advanced liberal strategy of governance. Much of the analysis thus far in this chapter and in the previous ones has traced the ways that neoliberal self-governing strategies are encouraged for criminalized women, both by the criminal justice system and by the alternative justice programs. Individuals are exhorted to work on themselves in order to transform their identity and behaviour into neoliberal ones. However, technologies of the self, as Foucault outlines them and as feminist authors have interpreted them, are much more fluid than this allows for (Vintges 2012). Though the techniques are always entwined with dominant mentalities, they are never simply reflections of those mentalities. Foucault discusses them as points of resistance to relations of power. Through technologies of the self, one can transform in ways that are non-normalizing so as to work against dominant norms, subjectivities, and relations of power (Taylor 2004). This aspect of self-governance, self-care, has been under-examined by criminologists.

In his analysis of Greek ethics and techniques of the self, Foucault (1994) argues that a crucial half of a well-known maxim has been lost in modern techniques. While the Greeks were concerned with the task of "knowing thyself," this task was fulfilled in order to "care for thyself." Feminist scholars built on this, arguing that care involves being attentive to and strengthening one's potential and capacities (McWhorter 1999). Caring for the self means knowing and transforming the self (McLaren 2002). It is a form of care that creates different subjectivities but that does so within power relations; "in this way, care of the self provides a way of using disciplinary practices in emancipatory ways" (O'Grady 2004, 110). The practices that constitute care of the self may look like neoliberal self-governing strategies as there is no outside of power. We can only start from where we are, and that means that technologies of the self will draw on, or "are always in some way imbricated within or modulated by[,] contemporary practices or existing (though not necessarily dominant) patterns of behavior"

(Lloyd 1996, 246). The governing practices engaged in by the programs under study are more than neoliberal governing strategies because of the ethic of care mentality and the radically different subject that is the subject to be known.

Techniques of the self and practices of self-care each focus on knowing the self; however, as mentioned above, they do so for varying purposes. The data show that participants mention two reasons one should engage in self-reflection: (1) to be in compliance with the neoliberal responsibilizing imperative ("know yourself so as to not commit crime") and (2) to increase your well-being ("know yourself so as to care for yourself"). One participant identified capacity building as a central tenet of the program: "I think that's a big feature that we provide, is that they actually see the potential that they have that they didn't realize. It's unrealized potential. We try to draw that out of them" (Caitlin). That potential, Caitlin continues, is then directed towards what the women themselves want: "We're going to be building the future, you know, in terms of having our women go out there and know exactly what it is that they want. Be strong and go out and ask for what they want properly and get it." Many of the participants' answers to my question "What is success for the program?" speak to the value they place on care work and on broadening the possibilities for the women. Consider this response from Kate: "Each person, whatever their, I see success in a lot of women. Even if it's a small thing. And it's just that baby step forward to growth. Because it could be a short time later that they're going to grow again, take another step forward." The growth or transformation facilitated by the programs is framed as useful for the individual woman's person goals rather than simply for reducing recidivism or producing neoliberal subjects.

Heyes's (2007) study of weight loss programs exemplifies how practices can be both practices of discipline and practices of self-care. Heyes largely agrees with feminist analyses of dieting that critique the practice as a disciplinary one, as a practice that constructs women as docile bodies and limits their options. She points, however, to the generative aspects of dieting as well.

Women engage in goal setting, feel a sense of accomplishment, and are able to do things, some physical, some emotional, that they were not able to do before losing weight. Ultimately, Heyes finds that weight loss programs put these capacities to use in the process of weight loss and in the pursuit of the project of normative femininity: "only losing weight, they would have us believe, can lead to true self-knowledge, self-development, self-mastery, and self-care" (86). But, crucially, they do not have to do this. She argues that women in the weight loss programs often had a critical awareness that led them to reject the all-encompassing disciplinary project of their specific program, Weight Watchers, and that this awareness allowed "the possibility of uncoupling new capacities from docility, and of recruiting those capacities to care of the self" (87). Heyes cites a number of capacities encouraged through her own participation in Weight Watchers, including sharing with groups of women, attentiveness to her own behaviours and patterns, and learning how to bring together communities of women for a common purpose. She argues that these could all be put towards purposes that resist dominant practices and discourses. Though the contexts are significantly different, I want to argue here that a similar possibility is present in the alternative justice programs. The capacities generated by the programs are not just useful in the construction of the neoliberal subject: they can also be put to use by the marginalized woman as practices of care. In many ways, the program staff encouraged this usage.

One particular capacity that the programs should strive to develop for the women to whom they are directed is the ability to link individual struggles to social context. Program staff do this in how they constitute the marginalized woman, but they also need to share that analysis with the criminalized woman herself. Some programs are currently doing this. This type of sharing and teaching a critical perspective is strongest in the Aboriginal programs. Indigenous staff not only constituted the criminalized woman as the marginalized woman, they also overtly shared that analysis with program participants. A strong critical consciousness is a key component of mobilizing neoliberal practices as practices of care, and the programs need to ensure they are developing this capacity in the women with whom they work.

The strong presence of care discourses changes how the justice practices engaged in by participants can be analyzed. In many respects, it seems as though the personal development programs discussed above employ quintessential neoliberal self-governance strategies. When they are read contextually, however, beside the construction of the criminalized woman as marginalized and alongside the ethic of care, they look different. Providing education, job training, and programming that assists in building self-esteem can also be interpreted as meeting the self-defined needs of criminalized women.

Focusing on self-defined needs, rather than on justice system needs, assists in building critical capacities and a resistant subject. Multiple studies working with criminalized women in the post-release context identify education, training, and support services as sorely needed (Allspach 2010; Baldry 2013; Kilroy et al. 2013). One of the strengths of Maidment's (2006a) research lies in the centrality she gives to the voices of criminalized women. The women in her study all speak to the pressing need for safe, affordable housing. Beyond the simple need for a place to live, Maidment also notes that "managing to secure decent accommodations can often mean the difference between staying out [of jail] during that first few months of release and going back inside" (104). She stresses the need for culturally specific programming for Indigenous women and notes an almost total lack of such programming. Maidment also finds a lack of gender-specific programming and concludes that community programming does not offer women the support they need to combat the structural oppressions with which they are faced. It is in this focus that her work and mine are congruent. My findings, however, paint a very different picture of the services available for criminalized women, as the agencies in Winnipeg are striving to meet many of the needs that the women in Maidment's study identify.

Even when there are programs that are striving to meet their care needs, women are often unfamiliar with existing community supports (Pollack 2009). The extensive referral work in which participants engage assists in this regard. Criminalized women in Pollack's study (2009) spoke to a general lack of information about, and unease in navigating, criminal justice, welfare, and other systems. Participants mentioned this as a constant concern. Much of the advocacy work they do involves explaining various official processes and assisting women with various bureaucracies. Emily described assistance she has given women both with Child and Family Services and Employment and Income Assistance:

> So oftentimes we assist women in getting lawyered up, for lack of a better word, so that they can get stuff before the court, to know what's going on ... There are some women in the community that come in and talk to me because I used to work in child welfare. So I'll assist them ... So what we try to do is get the EIA appointment for them when they're released. If they see us in jail we'll do that linkage. We'll make that appointment. So when they get out they have their appointment, so they don't have to wait.

Again, analyzed out of context, both of these functions – referral services and assisting in official processes – could be interpreted as responsibilizing the community, which, in turn, responsibilizes the women to be active individuals who take control of their own criminal and community justice processing. However, because the staff understand the criminalized woman to be marginalized and respond to her with notions of support and care, these strategies take on a different meaning. Staff are meeting women's needs, providing them with support and empowering them to know and exercise their rights. Staff assist women in making claims on the state, in gaining access to services to which they are entitled as citizens.

Initially, the programs' emphasis on work and training stood out as an exemplar of neoliberal strategy. Even this focus, however, can change when put in the larger discursive context of the interviews. Haney (2010) analyzes "work" as it is conceptualized in two women's prisons, one in Hungary and the other in the United States. The Hungarian prison puts wage labour at the centre of its programming, and work is seen as a right, a responsibility, and a way of building collectivity. Work in the American prison is not seen as wage labour; instead, it is conceptualized as an individual psychological process. In comparing the two prisons, Haney argues that work functions as a governing strategy in both cases, but that in Hungary it guides women towards social inclusion and collective good while in the United States it turns women away from the social and towards the personal work of the psyche. She concludes that "to the extent that prison labor leads to an awareness of women's social contributions, it might actually serve as an alternative to, as opposed to a reflection of, dominant forms of social exclusion" (94). Young (1994) argues that meaningful work is a key element of programs that aim to go beyond disciplining women to empowering them. The personal development programs offered by the agencies under study here can also be interpreted as offering something more than just the ability to become an active, responsible citizen. Work, education, and skills development, when mobilized along with a structural understanding of marginalization, can provide women with the ability to meet their own goals. The skills they acquire could be put to use in bettering their families and communities or simply in expanding their individual capabilities.

Like the concept of work, the concept of empowerment can be utilized in different ways. The governmentality literature emphasizes the use of empowerment in neoliberal governance (Cruikshank 1999). But the concept retains its social justice, feminist meaning as well: "the development of a sense of collective influence over the social conditions of one's life" (Young 1994, 48). According to the data I gathered, it is difficult to know to what extent this is actually accomplished. I cannot say that the criminalized women who go through these programs emerge with a sense of their commonalities as a group and their influence on the social conditions of their lives. But, because of the staff's construction of the criminalized woman as a socially situated, constrained subject, there is certainly the potential for empowerment. This understanding leads staff to recognize the "*social* aspects of disempowerment" that Pollack (2000, 86) argues is necessary when thinking about criminalized women. She recommends that prison programming adopt three strategies to enhance the development of empowerment: (1) the use of peer networks (discussed further below); (2) links with the community, which the alternative justice programs provide; and (3) chances for criminalized women to make their own links between their personal problems and social conditions – something the programs here should offer. The mobilizing public advocacy work in which most of the agencies examined here participate contributes to this potential. Their collective public advocacy work, sometimes with each other and often with other social service agencies, models and involves criminalized women in making changes to social conditions.

The inclusion of women who have successfully completed the program or who have lived experience of criminalization also contributes to the ability of the agencies' programs to empower women. In discussing the use of peer networks, Pollack (2009, 93) argues that, "by centering the knowledge and subjectivities of criminalized women, peer networks (organizations, supports, and advocates) carry the potential to redefine spaces of community for women leaving prison." Several of the agencies use peer support workers. Kihiw Iskewock Lodge has peer mentors, and both New Directions' TERF and the Salvation Army involve women with lived experience of criminalization. Their programs consistently centre the knowledge and subjectivity of the marginalized woman; they focus on the needs of women, drawn from the experiences of the women with whom they work. By focusing on the marginalized woman, care and support redefines the work the programs do, moving it away from neoliberal governing strategies and towards strategies of care for the self.

This redefinition takes place when strategies are coupled with an ethic of care. An ethic of care centres, validates, and strives to meet the criminalized woman's needs, while recognizing the social context within which they arise. An ethic of care is political: part of recognizing needs is the determination of who should be responsible for fulfilling them. This involves a critical awareness of social context and relationships. Tronto (1993, 177) argues that "care is a way of framing political issues that makes their impact, and concern with human lives, direct and immediate." So long as this framing is explicitly articulated alongside the caring practice, thus allowing criminalized women to develop their own critical attentiveness, an ethic of care transforms strategies of personal development into techniques of self-care.

The subject that participants constituted is multifaceted. It is a self that is not overdetermined by a woman's criminalized status as she is connected to and marginalized by social structures and bureaucracies. The marginalized woman, and the work she can do on herself, does not revolve around her criminalized behaviour; instead, the justice programs work with the criminalized woman to help her develop a number of capacities that will help her cope with oppressive social structures. These capacities are understood differently, and service different goals, than the narrow neoliberal goals of responsibilization and reducing recidivism.

Technologies of the self focus on a variety of goals. Sometimes the goal is to provide material and basic support; other times it is to assist in the building and sustaining of relationships. As Veronica commented about one woman: "So she [a resident] had her baby. The baby is in CFS care but with her. Residing with her, with us – again, 24/7 staff – which I'm glad to see not another child going to CFS as an infant and have a family screwed up for another nineteen years." Other times the goal is simply pleasure: "They can still laugh and smile and, you know, we take them horseback riding and whatever and they're giggly eight-year-old girls. We paint their nails and it's like a pajama party" (Sarah). The staff offer women strategies of self-care not only to induce responsibilization but also to allow them to survive and to potentially thrive. Although Caitlin is discussing the mandatory training aspect of the program, which is a good example of how women are responsibilized to become good neoliberal subjects, her rationale speaks to something more:

> For me, personally, I would just like them to take something. You know, whatever it is, if it's the friendship, if it's the fellowship, if it's the cooking, the going out, you know, and meeting new people, going on adventures, doing all these things. I want them, because I have, I just want everybody to be happy. You know what I mean? I want everybody to go out there and enjoy the word because we're only given one life.

The criminalized woman is not simply a neoliberal subject; therefore, these community programs cannot simply reflect neoliberal governance strategies.

This is especially true in yet another type of work in which the programs engage, what I have labelled "culture work." Three of the agencies are Aboriginal organizations and all (except for Mediation Services) integrate Indigenous traditions, teachings, and ceremony into their programming. I am uneasy about providing my observations on this aspect of the programs' work. I am a white settler Canadian, and, as such, I do not have an Indigenous worldview. Though my participants outlined the challenges Indigenous people face in a colonial world, they did not – nor did I ask them to – explain their Indigenous worldviews. I present some of the differences in their mentalities and strategies hesitantly, as there is much I could get wrong in doing so. I draw on leading Indigenous scholars in Canada to link the work done in these programs to larger projects of Indigenous resurgence. I try to carefully think about and answer questions that Nishnaabeg scholar Leanne Simpson poses and works through. As she draws on black feminist theory, she asks, "Can we [Indigenous scholars] ethically engage these bodies of work and struggle?" She answers: "I think my Nishnaabeg ethical practices demonstrate that I must develop relationships of reciprocity and coresistance with these communities that embody our ethical practices of solidarity. I cannot just *take* their theories" (Simpson 2017, 66, emphasis in the original).

White settlers must ask the same of our use and engagement with Indigenous work. The ethical use of Indigenous scholarship, and the ethics of doing this analytic work on Indigenous worldviews, troubles me more than my fear of simply getting it wrong. However, it is vital to show the presence of these ideas in alternative justice program work as it demonstrates that these spaces are not completely saturated by neoliberal mentalities. In the brief discussion that follows, I hope to highlight the important, culturally grounded work that programs are doing without positioning myself as an "expert" on that work or on Indigenous frameworks or knowledge.[1] Interested readers are encouraged to look at the large body of work being done in Canada and elsewhere by Indigenous scholars.

The first thing to note is that the label I have given this work is not ideal. I do not mean to suggest that the programs are engaging in "cultural" activities in ways that can be bracketed out from other political or material practices. This is important for, as Simpson (2017) notes, if we are referring only to things such as music, dance, and art, then Indigenous "culture" can take place within settler colonialism. This type of cultural expression becomes simply one of many that take place with a "multicultural" Canada. Simpson argues that, for Indigenous thought, "the cultural and the political are joined and inseparable" (49). The alternative justice programs are working through culture to reinforce Indigenous ways of knowing, thinking, and being. This is both political work and relational work. Through a variety of practices, the programs are teaching and practising an Indigenous framework:

> So, coming to a place like this and doing the smudging and going and doing the medicine picking, you know what I mean. They're all teachable moments and it's all really exciting. It's just embracing whatever it is. So, I guess that would be probably one of our biggest philosophies is following those seven teachings and most definitely respect.
>
> Because it's like you can smudge anywhere here, there are some pipe carriers on staff so that if you wanted a ceremony,

> this year we're trying to have regular sweats because [for] a lot of the women it's about the culture.
>
> We'll talk about grandmother moon and all that comes with that. We'll talk about maybe full moon ceremony or we'll talk about, we all wear dresses. And I have a whole pile of skirts back there. I ask them to put them on. We will [talk] about the importance of the skirt ... I can only talk about my teachings and the way I understand, and so I talk about that. And so that they know why they're wearing what they're wearing. Maybe they have some other reasons, you know, or maybe they have some other teachings and I open it up to, I don't know everything. So, you know, if we start talking about things maybe we'll understand it more. So, I invite them to talk about these things. See how they see how they see it. Yeah.
>
> The Elder at Kihiw Iskewock Lodge will work with the residents providing traditional teachings, sharing circles, and ceremonies to facilitate healing and transformation amongst the residents.

Although most of the agencies made some reference to taking a holistic look at the woman's life, the Aboriginal agencies made many specific references to the notion of balance. The work they do with criminalized women is focused on creating balance: "You have to have balance in [your] mental, physical, and emotional [life] as well" (Emily); "Well I think it's more restoring balance in somebody's life at the end of the day. I wouldn't even say making the wrongs right. I wouldn't say that, just, even if it's just a small step, just restoring some kind of balance in this person's life" (Mike). Balance was discussed as something the staff sought for the well-being of the woman; her equilibrium was for her sake.

Through this culture work, the criminalized woman is offered a new "Way of Being." This is the name of one of Onashowewin's workshops (which focuses on cultural teaching and ceremony), but it stands as an excellent descriptor of much of the work being done by the agencies. Offered to the criminalized woman, through teachings, history, and practices, is a way to know herself within a broader historical and cultural context. The programs offer the women the opportunity to ground themselves in an Indigenous worldview. Ariel stressed the importance of this: "Culture is the heartbeat of the program. Everybody is always learning." Similarly, Andrea explained:

> It helps them to see that they can make changes in their lives by recognizing how they came to be where they are, okay. You need to look back in order to do that. Now we like to do that culturally based because we need to look back far enough to who our people are. We need to take their values and bring them to our present time. In order to truly value ourselves or to know our identity, in order to know what we're about. And, you know, because we've been in poverty, we've been dislocated from our homes, our land, from all of these things over the past five hundred years, that's why we need to go back far enough to find out our true identity, which makes us stronger, without all of these things that were put upon us.

Not only do the programs make room for this culture work, its presence potentially changes aspects of the governing mentalities I have identified as neoliberal- or care-focused. The concept of responsibility, for example, takes on a different meaning when grounded in Indigenous culture. As Patricia Monture-Angus (1995, 28) argues, "responsibility as a basis for the structure of a culturally based discourse focuses attention not on what is mine, but on the relationship between people and creation (that is both the individual and collective)." Monture-Angus sets the concept of responsibility within a broader, culturally specific, and relational way of being. Here individual women's struggles are necessarily put into a collective context because they are seen through a worldview that, as Monchalin (2017) explains, understands people as always being part of a complex web of relationships – not only with each other but also with non-human others. We can see this relational focus and its connection to individual responsibility in Andrea's quote (above). In addition, while her focus remains on knowing the self, as highlighted by her rhetorical question to me – "Without understanding themselves or knowing who they are how can they make changes?" – that self is radically different from the neoliberal self. It is a subject – the Indigenous woman – that is resistant to assimilative, individualistic neoliberal governmentalities. It is an Indigenous subject who refuses the settler colonial project of removal.[2] It is a subject who can learn new capabilities and form new relationships that allow her to flourish. When we take the culture work the programs do seriously, this self is situated within a very different frame of understanding than what is allowed for by neoliberalism.

In this chapter I have examined how alternative justice staff think about the work they do with criminalized women. I have drawn both from their descriptions of the work they do and from their reflections to identify two mentalities of governance. A neoliberal mentality is present in much of the programming offered by the agencies – in particular, the personal development programming aims at encouraging criminalized women to be responsible, self-governing citizens. Alongside this there is an ethic of care mentality. Much of what the program staff do is care work, which largely consists of identifying and meeting the needs of criminalized women.

The practices in which the programs engage are always governing practices. They are employed to order the conduct of criminalized women and they can both reinforce dominant mentalities and support the construction of a resistant self. They can be read as governing women in a way that is consistent with neoliberal governance as well as in a way that is consistent with an ethic of care. Veronica described the struggles of her staff: "We struggled with the whole feminist philosophy of helping and empowering women versus implementing an oppressive judicial system." For the agencies in this study, it is not a matter of helping versus controlling: it is both.

The fact remains that, even if the alternative justice initiatives offered by these community agencies provide criminalized women with care and techniques of self-care, this is done in a coercive manner. Women participate in these programs because they are mandated to do so by the criminal justice system. This means that, notwithstanding their aims, mentalities, and ethic, the programs are also about reducing crime. This fact, coupled with the multiple and conflicting themes of the programs, complicate the degree to which they are alternative.

4

Alternative Justice? Resisting Criminal Justice Mentalities and Practices

> Yes we'd like it [the criminal justice system] to change. How can you get that to change? You know, maybe the only way is to advocate something different. Does that make sense?
>
> (Emily)

THE GOVERNMENTALITY LITERATURE has mainly looked at cases wherein practices of the self and strategies of governance operate in tandem "with state practices fitting seamlessly with practices of self-creation" (Bevir 2010, 425). But what happens when they look different? What happens when neoliberal mentalities are present beside social justice mentalities and when neoliberal technologies of the self can also be deployed as techniques to care for the self? Potential space opens for both program staff and criminalized women to resist neoliberal governance strategies and different ways of doing justice become possible. This resistance, however, is local, fragile, and constrained. It is a struggle for the staff, who can easily slide back into dominant governing mentalities. And, of course, there is no guarantee that criminalized women will take up these practices as a form of resistance.

Resistance is generally a marginal part of the analysis of neoliberalism (Leitner et al. 2007). Here, I analyze material examples of resistance. I begin with a theoretical discussion of resistance, which is perhaps the most contentious, and yet crucial, concept in poststructural feminism. I look at the ability of poststructural feminism to discuss, define, and achieve resistance. How might we act against and think differently about dominant discourses and practices? I then turn to the empirical. How does alternative justice resist? The bulk of the chapter looks at the multiple ways that resistance is present in the alternative justice programs I studied. I cannot say that these programs are offering to criminalized women an entirely different type of justice, but I can examine the ways in which different work, subjects, and mentalities coalesce to allow for the possibility of resisting the criminal justice system.

Resistance in Theory

Can/Should We Resist?

It is necessary to go beyond the governmentality literature in order to theorize resistance to the neoliberal framing of and response to the criminalized woman. While this literature has amassed a detailed body of work tracing the emergence and spread of neoliberal governance, it has had very little to say about resistance to that governance. Balfour (2006) criticizes governmentality analyses for not offering clear, pragmatic solutions to neoliberal governance and suggests that this lack of answers makes governmentality, and poststructural approaches more generally, an untenable and even dangerous theory for feminism. I concur with Balfour's assessment that governmentality scholars have not offered solutions; indeed, I would go further to argue that they have not offered theoretically helpful ways of seeing resistance even when it exists.

This is a criticism with which Rose, O'Malley, and Valverde (2006) take issue. They argue that governmentality studies are "full of accounts of conflicts and struggles ... rival programs and strategies" (100). Their choice of language here, along with their distinguishing governmentality as "critical, but not critique" (ibid.), speaks to the main issue governmentality encounters in relation to resistance: the absence of normative standards, a refusal to make value judgements. This is a critique that feminists have made of Foucault's work in general. Feminists are highly critical of what they see as a complete lack of normative assumptions in

Foucault's work (McNay 1992; Ransom 1993). The most generous analysis identifies Foucault as "normatively confused" (Fraser 1989, 31). Foucault (1991, 84) openly refuses to posit any ideas around "what is to be done." For Foucault, it is not our job as scholars to correct the problems that we identify. While providing detailed descriptions of discourse and subject formation, Foucault "refrains from problematizing the normative validity of power/knowledge regimes" (21). This is highly problematic for feminist theory.

Foucault's lack of a normative framework is a problem for feminist theory because "feminists *do* need to make normative judgements and to offer emancipatory alternatives" (Fraser 1995, 71, emphasis in original). The foundation of feminist theory is that women are oppressed *and* that oppression should end. Attentive to difference and to the particularities of oppression, feminists start from the general argument that women's exclusion and oppression exist, making feminism a value-laden framework in so far as it argues that this oppression is wrong. Feminist theory rests on the positive value of the emancipation of women. Scholars such as Soper (1993) argue that Foucault's work does not allow us to even articulate, let alone work towards, those emancipatory goals. Some feminists argue that Foucault, in his lack of normative judgements, has nothing to offer a feminist future (Grimshaw 1993).

Those feminists who believe Foucault's work can be useful for feminism have rebutted this criticism. They argue that Foucault's commitment to scepticism and critique, his questioning of norms, discourses, and the present, are all enough to allow for the type of social change that feminist theory encourages (Amigot and Pujal 2009; Taylor and Vintges 2004). McLaren (2002, 35) argues that Foucault's "scepticism about norms is a form of critical engagement with social and political issues." These theorists turn, in particular, to Foucault's late work and argue that the ethic of the self that he proposes allows for politics as a personal ethos (see various contributors to Taylor and Vintges 2004).

While I concur with those critical of Foucault that we need a normative foundation in order to do feminist work, I follow

Foucauldian feminists in thinking about how we should do so. Certainly, Foucault and those who use his work point to the dominant and harmful uses of principles such as justice and freedom; they do not, however, see these principles as inherently oppressive. Sawicki (1991, 100–1) argues that, in the absence of alternative standards of critique, we must utilize those that are available in our present context: "In other words appeals to rights, liberties, and justice (and struggles over how to interpret these principles) are not denied to us. These are the only sorts of appeals that make sense to us right now." We can appeal to the normative criteria available to us, while recognizing that they are specific to this social moment. She acknowledges that this was not a tactic Foucault utilized but argues that there is nothing in his approach that stops feminists from doing so. This is a similar argument to the one made by Fraser (1989). Allen (2011, 55), too, argues that we can use our norms and values to make normative judgements: "the proviso is that we must be suitably modest and contextualist about the status of our idealizations, and open to the possibility that they will one day be revealed, in the lights of historical and cultural developments that we cannot now envision, to be dangerous illusions rather than harmless idealizations." Foucault's unwillingness to appeal, explicitly, to these standards what limits him as a source for conceptualizing resistance.

In this book I approach the neoliberal governance of criminalized women as something that contributes to women's unjust social oppression. I do so, however, while attempting to remain vigilant regarding my own feminist-based power and strategies for thinking about women's oppression. I want to make the Foucauldian-inspired point that it is necessary to constantly interrogate any given normative judgement. We must use the normative standards we have while recognizing that they are not infallible.

What Is Resistance?

When speaking directly of resistance, Foucault has little to offer beyond a cursory description of resistance as co-constitutive of power, so I draw on feminist uses of his work that engage more directly with the concept. Like power, resistance must be seen as local and transitory, and it is never outside of the power that it resists. For Foucault, resistance does not have to be a grand, totalizing end point. Even those feminist theorists who use Foucault note that his theorizing on resistance is underdeveloped (Bartky 1988; Haber 1996: Sawicki 1991). This is in keeping with Foucault's general hesitancy to be prescriptive or to offer solutions. His greatest contribution to thinking about resistance is in his illustration of the ways in which philosophers, scholars, and thinkers generally resist. In order to expand the potential for resistance to individuals, groups, and movements, the work of Foucauldian feminists – and those who critique this approach – is essential.

Feminists have drawn not only on Foucault's few remarks about resistance but also on various parts of his oeuvre – such as his genealogical approach (Sawicki 1996); his approach to philosophy as lived critique (Heyes 2007; McWhorter 1999); and, as I discuss in detail below, his techniques of the self – to construct a theory of resistance that can be put to work within a feminist framework. This is, perhaps, the most contentious part of Foucault's thinking for feminists: whether or not one can, as an individual or as a group, resist.

Many feminist scholars argue that, because of his conception of power, resistance is not possible within a Foucauldian framework (Harstock 1990). If power is everywhere, they argue, resistance cannot take place. If there is no outside of power from which to resist, there can be no resistance. Foucauldian feminists rebut this argument by focusing on Foucault's claim that resistance is constitutive of power (Macleod and Durrheim 2002). The potential for resistance is omnipresent, and its exercise is central to power relations. Without resistance, power would cease to exist. Freedom, however small or constrained, is a necessary prerequisite to power relations (Foucault 1994).

Foucault's unwillingness to see potential in a mass revolution is another point of contention for feminist scholars. They argue that his position is nihilist. If there can be no overthrow of power, no end to power relations, then there is little point in struggling against them. Foucauldian feminists argue vigorously against this claim. First, they contend that there can be coordinated resistance. Mass resistance can be conceptualized in a manner similar to that discussed for power. Though there is no overarching source of power, power relations can be patterned; correspondingly, while there is no final overthrow of power, relations of resistance can become linked. Local instances of resistance can become patterned; they can spread, and they can cause cracks in dominant discourses. Second, the lack of guarantee of a complete revolution should not be enough to stop us from recognizing and struggling against unjust power relations.

Feminists also point out that Foucault's theory of the subject prohibits resistance. If there is no subject, they argue, there is no agency. If we are only ever the effects of power, how can we ever resist that power? They argue that Foucault's account of subjugation negates any possibility of resistance. However, if we take seriously Foucault's claim that freedom is necessary for power, then there must be room for subjects to move in an autonomous way (see my discussion of Allen [2011] in Chapter 2). In arguing for the agency of subjects I do not mean to suggest that they can simply and freely choose to resist. To do so would be to uncritically recreate the autonomous individual that is at the heart of neoliberal discourses. The subject is constituted not simply by one disciplinary discourse but by many; thus, while subjects may be constituted as docile, they are at the same time produced as able and with agency (Sawicki 1991). Subjects are constituted with the potential for resistance because "to be constituted by language is to be produced within a given network of power/discourse which is open to resignification, redeployment [and] subversive citation from within" (Butler 1995, 135). The power and discourse that make up the subject are complex: they are also contestable. In Foucault's relational conception of power, individuals are not only the effects of power, they are also its vehicles (McLaren 2002; Sawicki 1991).

The approach I take here is one that is exemplified by Evans, Riley, and Shankar (2010) and their contribution to the debates around agency and sexualization, particularly relating to young women. The authors insert their work into a debate played out in a series of articles on young women, clothing choices, sexuality, and agency (Duits and van Zoonen 2006; Gill 2007; Duits and van Zoonen 2007). In their 2006 article, Duits and van Zoonen examine two very different clothing options: the headscarf and "porno-chic" clothing. They argue that one of the clear aspects of both options is the erasure of the girls' agency in wearing them. They argue that it is necessary to "treat girls as capable and responsible agents, who produce 'speech acts' with their choice of clothing" (Duits and van Zoonen 2006). Gill (2007) writes a critical response, arguing that Duits and van Zoonen's (2006) analysis erases cultural context and valorizes the notion of the autonomous individual of neoliberalism. In a rejoinder, Duits and van Zoonen (2007) are critical of what they see as Gill's refusal to grant young women agency that she claims for herself. They also ask: "What does feminism gain – politically and analytically – by immediately countering any girl's or woman's appeal to autonomy by pointing out her false consciousness and putting her under all the constraints of patriarchy and capitalism?" (168).

It is within this context that Evans, Riley, and Shankar (2010) offer a Foucauldian-inspired discussion of agency that draws on technologies of the self to argue that the subject must take up discourses and, in so doing, can subvert them. Evans, Riley, and Shankar focus on practices of sexuality, things such as burlesque, pole dancing, and porno-chic clothing. They argue that young women adopting sexually suggestive clothing such as T-shirts that read "Porn Star" are resisting dominant discourses around passive female sexuality. At the same time, however, dominant discourses around age, race, body shape, and presentation of self mean that not every young woman can wear such a T-shirt. For an older, racialized woman or a younger woman whose body does not fulfill dominant shape and size standards, this choice will likely be met with derision rather than read as resisting docile body discourses. In examining how women can subvert and enact what they call "technologies of sexiness," Evans, Riley, and Shankar (2010) add two important constraints to agency: "the limitations imposed on who may participate in these practices, and ... how they are read by others" (124). Their analysis provides a nuanced example of how subjects take up discourses in multiple but not infinite ways. The important point here in terms of alternative justice programs is to acknowledge that resistance, and the agency to enact it, is possible but constrained.

Resistance, in a Foucauldian feminist approach, is refusal. It is the identification and refusal of the ways dominant discourses have constituted and responded to us as subjects – a refusal of what we are and how we know and are known at this moment. Resistance is an opening of possibility and "of transforming political relations through the production of new discourses and so new forms of power and new forms of the self" (Ramazanoglu 1993, 24). While this is generally how the Foucauldian approach to resistance is conceptualized, Lloyd (1996, 243) goes further and uses Foucault's writing on technologies of the self to argue that resistance is a "two course strategy." The first course is in the refusal to be what we are (or what we are perceived to be); the second is in the creation of new subjectivities and new ways of being and acting.

How neoliberal mentalities know and constitute the criminalized woman and how neoliberal practices respond to this have to be refused, and new possibilities need to be offered. The constitution of the criminalized woman as a neoliberal subject and the corresponding response to this individualizes and responsibilizes her. This is a problem since criminalized women's offending behaviour can only be understood by examining the ways in which their lives and behaviour are structured and constrained by gender, race, and class. Holding them personally responsible for actions taken while constrained in these ways perpetuates the oppression of women as a group. In order to imagine justice differently we must refuse the dominant responses and create new responses and subjects.

Resistance in Alternative Justice Programs

The alternative justice programs I investigated are spaces of resistance as the discourse used by the participants contains versions of the criminalized woman that are at odds with that offered by the criminal justice system. The dominant construction of criminalized women solely as neoliberal subjects is refused while, at the same time, the different subjects on offer provide multiple ways of being. Resistance is present in the multiplication of subjectivities. The women in these programs interact with three different versions of the criminalized woman – the neoliberal subject, the psychologized woman, and the marginalized woman – and this increases the possibilities for subjectivity. The women may take on whichever version or versions they feel is most useful to them. In order to meet their own objectives, they can strategically play to certain aspects of the neoliberal subject, the psychologized woman, or the marginalized woman.

The simple presence of multiple forms of subjectivity is an act of resistance. It splinters the criminalized woman and creates room for agency and for difference. As a way of practising freedom, McWhorter (1999, 181) argues that we need "disciplinary practices that we might engage in carefully, deliberately, but with modifications that militate against standardized outcomes." That potential lies in alternative justice. In alterative programs, criminalized women are offered some movement in terms of identity, in contrast to the formal system, wherein they are constituted, understood, and responded to as neoliberal subjects.

Beyond being facilitated by the multiplicity of identity that these programs allow, resistance is also facilitated through the specifics of the other subjects. There are features of the marginalized woman and psychologized woman that directly refuse some of the more problematic aspects of the neoliberal subject. They work as "forms of the subject that are capable of functioning as resistance to the normalizing power" (Oksala 2005, 190). Understanding the psychologized woman to act as a result of her illness(es) rather than as a result of free choice counters neoliberal ideas of individual responsibility. Making demands for medical facilities, doctors, and treatment centres has the potential to remove the criminalized woman from the criminal justice arena entirely. The discourse of the marginalized woman further refuses the trope of individual responsibility. The marginalized woman is wholly situated within her social context, directly resisting the decontextualization and individualization of neoliberal governance approaches. In both of these constructions – the psychologized woman and the marginalized woman – the gender neutrality of the neoliberal subject is challenged. Her experiences and identity as a woman are affirmed, and these experiences and this identity are then placed back into a social context. This point is tremendously important. In her analysis of community-based alternative residential centres, Haney (2010, 146) points out that one of the key problems with the programming was that staff "lost their social imaginations. Their discourses and practices led them to deny the social origins of their charges' problems." She argues that this loss of social imagination resulted in the staff exercising forms of control and punishment over the women in the program, and that the latter rejected this framing of their lives. For the alternative justice programs in Winnipeg to retain the necessary social imagination is a crucial point of resistance.

The Indigenous identity present in the programs is also a crucial source of resistance. Constituting the marginalized woman as Indigenous allows the programs to resist the neoliberal tendency to deny group identity and affiliation. It strongly positions the criminalized woman not as an individual but as a member of a collective. This identity is not only present in the discourse used by participants but also actively practised by many of the programs. The culture work done by the programs, and the Indigenous perspectives incorporated into the other types of work, strives to build and pass on to the women a strong Indigenous identity. This directly refuses the dominant discourses of settler colonialism, which deny and attempt to remove this identity. The form of resistance that is generated through the building and living of Indigenous identity is one that Indigenous peoples have deployed throughout the history of colonialism. These programs, where they consciously work to share Indigenous teachings, history, and culture, can be seen as enacting resistance by, in Alfred and Corntassel's (2005) terms, "being Indigenous." Several of the programs are engaged in "thinking, speaking and acting with the conscious intent of regenerating one's indigeneity" (614) and in sharing and strengthening that Indigeneity with the criminalized women with whom they work. Resistance here is found not simply in the offering of multiple subjectivities but in the particular Indigenous identity offered to criminalized women.

There are, of course, limits to the degree to which the programs offer a fluid notion of identity for criminalized woman. This is not a space of free-wheeling identity formation: no space can be. One limitation is that in constructing identities, staff are drawing on socially bounded understandings. Because of this, aspects of the alternatives offered by the programs may well reflect dominant and normative discourses. As Heyes (2007, 118) states, "resistance to these constraints, therefore, cannot simply invoke alternative substantive accounts of the kinds of subjects we would be better off being, since these accounts will have their own apparatus of normalization." The linking of womanhood to motherhood and what it means to be a good mother within the marginalized woman narrative, for example, may reproduce the patriarchal limiting of women to the role of mother and reinforce neoliberal ideas of the responsible mother. This discourse positions a child's well-being as dependent largely, if not wholly, on a mother who always puts her child's needs before her own (Minaker and Hogeveen 2015a). With regard to criminalized women who use drugs, Kilty and Dej (2012) trace the ways in which the identity of "good" mother is used both against and by them in ways that can reinforce stigma and increase the likelihood of their "failing" to meet expectations. While offering criminalized women the space to take up a discursive position that they are largely denied – that of the good mother – may be a powerful act of resistance, it may also reinforce ideas of personal responsibility. And it may change if the material conditions in which marginalized women mother are not modified. This is particularly true for Indigenous mothers. Landertinger (2015, 73) shows the ways in which "the Indigenous mother emerges as the archetypical 'bad mother' in the colonial imaginary" and argues that resistance and change will not be made within the structure of settler colonialism. To encourage Indigenous women to take up the position of good mother without altering the structure that produces the discursive and material conditions that criminalize Indigenous parenting keeps the focus narrowly tied to individuals.

Tying women's criminality to their bodies via medicalization poses the same danger, as does subjecting them to the "good mother" discourse. In explaining women's behaviour in direct reference to their medical conditions and psychological health, there is a risk that the criminalized woman will be wholly reduced to her body, a reduction against which feminist criminologists and feminists have fought (see, for example, Faith's [1993] discussion of the historical and modern tendencies to tie women to their biology; Comack and Brickey 2007). These dangers are more likely to be realized when staff members hold strict ideas about identity. Further study of alternative justice programs, particularly observational or ethnographic research, may be able to further explore the ways in which this is practised. Are there rigid boundaries on the various identities held out to criminalized women? Can a woman be the wrong kind of marginalized woman or psychologized woman or Indigenous woman? How do staff members respond to women who do not fit these categories? Finally, to what degree do staff and the program problematize the general identity of Woman?

It is important to remember that I am not identifying the marginalized woman as who the criminalized woman "really" is; rather, this is a feminist discursive construction often used by service providers. There are dangers in substituting a feminist subject for a neoliberal subject. Feminism has, in various ways throughout its history as a discipline and movement, constrained women by how it constructs them. McWhorter (1999, 2004) traces the initial creativity and sense of possibility she felt with woman-affirming practices – practices that questioned and refused patriarchal norms.

She argues, however, that these practices coalesced into the discovery of a feminist subject, and that this tended towards "a way of experiencing selfhood (and the world) that places stability over becoming and change, into a way of thinking that places knowledge over openness toward otherness and difference, toward that which eludes categorization" (McWhorter 2004, 152). The recent anti-trans positions taken by some feminists are a striking example of this (see the group Gender Identity Watch, which describes its contributors as "lawyers who apply a radical feminist analysis to gender" and are virulently anti-trans; Raymond 1994, 2015). The identity of a woman or a feminist in these examples is tightly bound and denies trans women's inclusion. Stability and certainty in that subject position result in the denial and exclusion of an entire group of women. The Winnipeg programs, with their intersectional approach and their belief that each woman must be responded to based on her needs, mitigate some of these dangers. They remain, however, and especially if these identities are held out as end points, as something that, once taken up, can be put out of mind rather than treated as forms of identity produced and reproduced through an ongoing process.

There are features of the governance mentalities that may allow for resistance, in addition to the resistant potential found in the multiplicity of subject positions. The discourse of care used by participants has resistant aspects because their focus on care meant that they broadened the identified needs of the criminalized woman well beyond the scope allowed for by neoliberal strategies. This discourse also has the potential to move discussions of responsibility away from focusing solely on individual responsibility towards focusing on collective responsibility. Diamond and Quinby (1988, 203) argue that, "whereas today bodies, skills, and pleasures are on the whole linguistically sexuated and scientized, discourses of caring and nurturance have the potential to challenge disciplinary power's claim to control." Again, and slightly contrary to Diamond and Quinby, I would argue that there is nothing inherently challenging about a discourse of care: an ethic of care is not inherently good and problem-free. For example, the mother-child relationship is often offered as the paradigmatic care relationship. Tronto (1993), however, outlines a number of dangers in it, including an attitude of paternalism/maternalism on the part of the caregiver. Those working from a feminist ethic of care warn of the assumptions about care inherent in the mother-child relationship – namely, that it is something done by women, in private, for no money, and solely for love. Several of the participants referenced the mother-child relationship when describing their work with criminalized women. By invoking the maternal relationship as the paradigmatic relationship of care, and thereby feminizing care, they risk depoliticizing women's relationships and work. It is thus important to note that, while the ethic of care is a discourse that can resist neoliberal values, it can also support them.

The Winnipeg programs offer space for the staff to resist and for resistant ideas to form. Resistance is also possible for the individual criminalized woman who participates in the programs. For her, the techniques of self-care have the potential to move beyond allowing resistance as refusal and to instead provide transformative practices. Feminists have interpreted techniques of the self as a way of practising freedom. We cannot remove ourselves wholly from relations of power to some place or state of being that is free. Thus, freedom is not, in this framework, an endpoint; rather, it is something that we practise. Freedom is practised in the second part of resistance identified by Lloyd (see above): the opening of space for new ways of being. The techniques of the self I discuss here and in the previous chapter are ways of practising freedom, "that is, they create new non-normalizing modes of existence and relationships" (McLaren 2004, 230). These practices are oriented towards self-transformation, resisting dominant forms of the self, and striving towards new possibilities (McLaren 2002). Women are able to act as agents of resistance as they come to understand and work on themselves in different ways. So long as the agencies incorporate this identity work into their programs, criminalized women can engage in practising freedom through "collective and individual 'work on the limits' of one's culture, inventing new subjectivities and self-techniques by critically re-working the present ones" (Vintges 2012, 7). It is, in part, through these techniques of self-care that a critical subject is constituted – a subject who is better able to resist the normalizing, responsibilizing mentality of neoliberalism. Foucauldian feminists have used this understanding of freedom and techniques of the self as a way of providing one potential strategy for action (an aspect of their critique that others have argued was lacking).

While Foucauldian feminists uphold practices of the self as the way of resisting normalizing power relations, other feminists are highly critical of this argument. For example, Grimshaw (1993) is critical of Foucault, arguing that, in his later works, he finds freedom in the practices that he long described as constraining, normalizing, and dominating. She goes on to argue that Foucault does not sufficiently explain this change and that this

> leads him to evade the crucial question of when forms of self-discipline or self-surveillance can with any justification be seen as exercises of autonomy or self-creation, or when they should be seen, rather, as forms of discipline to which the self is subjected, and by which autonomy is constrained. (66)

This same criticism may be levelled at my own analysis. I have argued that personal development programs and work are, at one and the same time, both neoliberal strategies and strategies that resist neoliberal discourse.

Theoretically, I contend that there may be no distinction between practices that are disciplinary and those that are resistant. Both must be empirically examined. What will differentiate them is critical reflection: the ability of the subject to reflect, to think, to critically deconstruct practices and their limits. In order to be acts of resistance, in order to be practices of freedom, these technologies require critical reflection as "the subject constituted by the power/knowledge network is now capable of turning back on itself: of critically studying the processes of its own constitution, but also subverting them and effecting changes in them" (Oksala 2005, 165). McLaren (2002) makes this point in her examination of autobiography as a practice of the self. She argues that autobiography can be a technology of the self that leads to transformation and that works as a practice of freedom. Autobiography can also operate as a technology of domination: it "can be either an exercise in subjection, if it produces the required truth about oneself, or it can be a process of subjectification, if one critically examines how one came to be as one is with reference to normalizing discourses" (152).

If the techniques of the self in the justice programs are to be resistant rather than neoliberal, then staff members have to encourage, and offer opportunities for, criminalized women to engage in critical examination. The potential for this seems greatest in the staff activities that go beyond justice work. The activist work conducted by staff members frames the work they do with criminalized women and enables them to make strong connections between individual women and their social context. This gives a different meaning to the practices they encourage the women to adopt. The strongest evidence that staff encourage criminalized women to engage in critical reflection occurs in the culture work aspect of the programs. In the teaching of history, tradition, and the practice of culture, the data show that staff overtly encourage women to think critically about themselves in relation to their Indigenous culture and the colonial context in which they live.

Feminists have offered two particular practices through which critical reflection and the resistant practise of the self may be fostered. Both can be incorporated relatively easily into the types of work done by alternative justice programs. The first practice is the classic feminist model of consciousness raising. In consciousness raising, group members reflect on their own experiences and link them to larger social conditions and discourses. In these spaces, modes of subjectivity and the "truths" that build them can be critiqued. The goal of consciousness raising as a resistant practice of the self "would not be to tell us who we are, but rather to free us from certain ways of understanding ourselves" (Sawicki 1991, 44). The alternative justice programs have a variety of programs that include groups. It may be that consciousness raising is included within some of them, but this was not noted in program documents or interviews. In any case, adding this component to the programs would enable women to practise and reflect on a variety of selves and thus could increase the potential for resistance.

The second practice offered by feminists is self-writing in the form of autobiography. There are two projects in the data that fulfill the purpose of self-writing. A participant from Kihiw Iskewock Lodge outlined one goal she had when she arrived at the Lodge:

> My vision was to do the teaching and take them out on outings and have them collaging their stay here. Taking pictures, you know, so they can remember the journey that they had. It's all part and parcel. We all meet for a reason. We're all put in each other's place for a reason. It's all teaching.

If it only serves as a vehicle for remembering, then collage making may not fulfill the requirements of critical reflection; however, it may fulfill them very well if women are encouraged to reflect on their journey as they engage in this activity. If women were given ample licence with regard to what they put together in their collage, and if they were given space and assistance in critically thinking about their journey, this process could be tremendously useful in encouraging resistant techniques of self.

Another project that slightly modified the practice of self-writing was a mannequin project conducted by the Salvation Army. Participants in multiple programs were given white plastic mannequins and asked what dignity meant to them. They then used various artistic media to build a subject indicative of dignity. Here we see the potential for women to generate a graphic representation of critical practices of the self. However, we also see the potential of the self being constructed in alignment with a narrow set of neoliberal (or in the case of the Salvation Army, religious) parameters.

Self-writing, as a practice, has both the potential to allow for critical reflection and the potential to encourage women to know themselves better so that they can work to become better neoliberal subjects. With this practice, as with all of the others I have examined, there is nothing inherently resistant or dominant about self-writing. In order to strengthen resistance, alternative justice programs could incorporate critical self-writing into their work. Staff could very well provide space for the women to develop a critical awareness of themselves and to engage in practices of self-care by encouraging them to think through and record who they are, how they have come to be where they are, who they want to be, and how to get there.

We can imagine, however, a form of self-writing that does not allow for this resistance. Indeed, the process by which some probation offices engage with their clients is a clear example of this. Upon entering the probation process offenders fill in a biography, providing a host of biographical details. Participants are encouraged to sit and reflect on important relationships in their lives, addictions, spending habits, and leisure activities as outlined in the template with which they are provided. This is not a free writing process; rather, it is focused by predetermined criminogenic risk factors. Staff assist in the writing by defining areas for the participant, pushing her to reveal more, and questioning her on aspects of the biography they suspect to be disingenuous. This information is then used by staff to construct the pre-sentence report and the conditions of probation. In this form of self-writing we see a clear example not of a practice of freedom but, rather, of a practice of neoliberal self-governance. The particular types of knowledge that are solicited by the template are based on neoliberal ideas about risk. This knowledge is generated in the service of neoliberal self-governance. The goal is not to refuse dominant ways of being or inspire new subjectivities or capacities for the individual: the goal is to make a plan that is set within the narrow parameters allowed by neoliberal crime strategies and that will reduce the risk that that individual will commit another crime.

Scholars have identified the use of self-writing as a neoliberal governance tool in other criminal justice contexts as well. LaCombe (2008) argues that the same logics and dominating tendencies appear in the self-writing that takes place in a prison-based sex offender treatment program. LaCombe conducted an ethnography of a cognitive-behavioural program for sex offenders in order to analyze treatment in the context of risk-based correctional logics. The goal of the program, in line with the neoliberal justice practice I describe throughout this book, is to produce rational, responsible individuals who make the good decisions necessary to manage their risk of reoffending. In order to do this, the sex offenders in LaCombe's research must be able to narrate their risks, their triggers, their fantasies, and their offences. This is done in individual sessions, group work, and through writing. One of the writing exercises the participants in the program must complete is a series of "Good Me/Bad Me" checklists in which they identify the conditions under which they do not offend and those under which they do. These are not the type of free and reflexive forms of self-writing that constitute a practice of freedom, as we might infer simply from their checklist form; instead "a lot of coaching goes into the task of creating the checklists, which are reviewed and corrected in the individual sessions with the therapists" (61). In a notebook and in group sessions these offenders must correctly identify and detail both appropriate and inappropriate sexual fantasies they have had. The boundaries between those that are acceptable and those that are not are created and enforced by the therapists to the point at which participants told LaCombe that they sometimes fabricated fantasies so that they could tell the staff what they want to hear. This program uses various self-writing tools to teach offenders to narrate their thoughts, feelings, fantasies, and actions in appropriate ways and, in so doing, to become responsible risk managers.

Similarly, McKim (2008) describes the confessional, "therapeutic" life reflection and writing that women had to undertake in a community alternative justice program for drug users. Participants had to share intimate details of their life in group sessions, therapy with counsellors, and in writing. These strategies replicate the ones used in the sex offender programming LaCombe studied and seem directed towards similar ends. As McKim argues, the program "involved rigorous, daily discussion and examination of one's emotions and painful past experiences, all of which were subject to analysis and judgment, with the goal of making this part of the self governable" (313). In order to try to ensure that self-writing remains resistant and does not become another neoliberal governance tool, the programs should strive not to engage in the type of coaching and judgment the authors describe above. They can also encourage criminalized women to share their writing with each other, perhaps in a forum organized by criminalized women or the peer workers whom some programs employ. This may allow women to "reveal the intimate details of their personal struggles to create a body of shared knowledge and to help others 'live through' similar experiences," which was how Ouellette and Arcy (2015, 106) found that the magazine writing they studied maintained a resistant ethos. This may also assist in addressing the criticism about the care of the self I describe below.

The focus on the subject and the self has been criticized by some as too individualistic a solution for feminism. Raby (2005) points to a lack of theorizing regarding how these resistant practices could be organized into something more collective. Allen (2011) too, though she sees much usefulness in Foucault's ideas, acknowledges that, while Foucault provides many important tools for thinking about politics and power, he does not address the collective dimension of the political. Sawicki (1996) argues, however, that these practices seem individualistic not because that is where they must remain but because they focus on the individual level of struggle. Similarly, O'Grady (2004, 111) argues that "care for the self provides a way of resisting and transforming the intra-subjective effects of given identities and the self-policing technologies that support and maintain them. In this light, greater care for the self can be seen as constituting political activity at the 'microphysical' level." This is not to deny the need for change at the macro level of broader discourses and social relationships. Although these practices start from the level of individual struggle they can be used as political practices. They are a powerful way to do the work that feminism has always done to link the personal to the political. Reflecting on the constitution of subjects and selves necessarily involves critiquing the social context in which they develop (McLaren 2002). This is one strategy of resistance, and it is one that can be coupled with collective strategies; indeed, for many, this is a necessary precondition for engaging in collective practices of resistance. The ability to reflect on and place ourselves within a critical framework then inspires and enables us to join others in making social change. As Ouellette and Arcy (2015, 102, emphasis in original) argue: "In the hands of women, queers, people of color, youth, and the economically disadvantaged attending to and caring for oneself can become a strategy of coping with and managing a racist, sexist, and homophobic society and for fashioning and re-fashioning resilient selves for the *longue durée* of social change." These practices allow resistance to move from the individual level to something that is broad-based, something that could change the relations within the justice complex.

That practices of self-care can be social practices, not simply individual ones, is not something that can be assumed: it must be shown. McNay (1992, 197) argues that a primary task for feminists is to show "how a politics of self-actualization need not lapse inevitably into introversion but may contribute to wider forms of progressive social change." With regard to criminalized women, however, many of them will need to address their own individual marginalization before they can even think about contributing to a social movement focused on ending social oppression. Practices of self-care and the building of a critically aware self will assist them in both of those endeavours. Though difficult to assess from the data, it could be that in offering practices of self-care and different subject positions, the Winnipeg programs assist the women and link their self-understanding and practices to collective action. The example of consciousness raising assists in this regard, helping the practices of self-care to become practices of the criminalized women as a group. This is not to say that these different subject positions, mentalities, and practices should not be interrogated – they should. They are not inherently better than any other, but resistance is fostered by their presence in so far as they contest the programs' neoliberal aspects. I am not arguing that the marginalized woman is the real criminalized woman or that an ethic of care is the proper or only response to her. These constructions contain their own limits and their own constraints on possibility. Nonetheless, from a feminist standpoint, their presence in the alternative justice programs is positive.

Practices of care of the self and subjectifying discourses must be interrogated empirically: "evaluating the political status of [these] practices should be a matter of historical and social investigation and not a priori theoretical pronouncement" (Sawicki 1991, 43). The subjectivities and the capacities generated by the programs do have resistant features, but it is only through close discursive examination that this can be known. Lloyd (1996, 250, emphasis in original) argues that it is not "the activity of self-fashioning in itself that is crucial. It is the way in which that self-fashioning, when allied to critique, can produce sites of contestation over the meanings and contours of identity, and over the ways in which certain practices are mobilized." Lloyd is referring to feminist analysis and a general feminist politics, which is precisely what I argue the programs are providing: practices of the self that are allied with critical reflections on the dominant criminal justice identities, norms, and practices. In so doing they are offering criminalized women space in which their capacities can be built and different possibilities can be created. The programs act as spaces of contestation and creation for criminalized women against and beyond what is allowed by neoliberal governance.

Despite feminist attempts to link these practices of critical care of the self to larger patterns of resistance, there are no clearly defined strategies for doing so. This is particularly true when the analysis moves beyond how we should work on ourselves to how we are with each other. As a personal ethos for the feminist philosopher, a critical care of the self seems like a good resistance strategy. How it becomes so for feminism as a social movement is less clear. This is a weakness of a Foucauldian approach that even those using it acknowledge. Heyes (2007, 133) points to this lacuna in Foucauldian theorizing and argues that more work needs to be done to explain how care of the self "can be a set of practices that includes an understanding of responsibility and ethical commitment to embodied others." In an extended analysis of the idea of freedom in Foucault's work, Oksala (2005) is critical of the lack of a relational aspect to techniques of the self. She argues that "the most fundamental ethical question does not concern my relationship to myself, but to the other" (195), and this means reversing how Foucault thinks about the ethical practices of the self.

In order to overcome this weakness in Foucault's thought and more clearly see how the practices of the self could lead to social change, I continue to draw on two bodies of feminist theory: Foucauldian feminism and a feminist ethic of care. McWhorter (2013) and Sawicki (2013) find much value in Foucault's idea of care of the self and refute the notion that these are individualistic practices. McWhorter argues that, because Foucault's notion of the subject is relational, so too are the practices of that subject. She insists that "a self comes to and continues to be in a network of social and political relations; selves do not exist without others. Caring for oneself involves caring for both known and unknown others in personal, communal, and civic relationships" (McWhorter 2013, 72). There is a case to be made, then, that there is nothing in the practice of the care of the self that stops it from being a collective practice. I draw on feminist ethic of care theorists and their incorporation of responsibility into the notion of care in order to strengthen that claim, in order to move care of the self from allowing to demanding collective resistance.

Throughout this book I discuss responsibility as a key neoliberal concept. The responsibility for preventing crime and for governing criminalized women is placed upon the community. The responsibility for making good choices, for engaging in proper conduct, is placed upon the individual. Neoliberalism, as a mode of governance, works to govern at a distance by encouraging others to take responsibility for governing themselves. Responsibility also enables resistance to neoliberalism if it is conceptualized as responsibility to others (Heyes 2007). If, rather than examining what we are encouraged to take responsibility for we instead look at what responsibility we have to others, then we may be able to link the individual practices of self-care to resistant social practices. McLaren (2002, 160) argues that "self-transformation can lead to social transformation as individuals create new non-normalizing, noninstitutionalized ways of living with and relating to one another." Integrating the idea of responsibility for meeting the caring needs of each other into this idea can increase the possibility that self-transformation leads to social change.

Rather than argue that the practices of care of the self *can* involve care of others, the feminist ethic of care theorists argue that it *does* and *should*. Responsibility is a crucial concept in the feminist ethic of care. Throughout her foundational text, Gilligan (1982, 73) describes the ethic of care as an ethic of responsibility and says that the women she studied saw the exercise of care "as the fulfillment of moral responsibility." We have a responsibility to care for each other because we are fundamentally relational beings. This echoes McWhorter's (2013) assertion, and the general Foucauldian feminist idea, that we are relational beings. Starting from the relational self, then, the ethic of care sees responsibility to those to whom we are connected as an imperative. Responsibility to care is a necessary part of care (Tronto 1993). If we apply this tenet to techniques of care of the self, then in taking care of the self one should also incorporate considerations of responsibility and care for others.

For Sevenhuijsen (2004), responsibility to care for everyone all the time is not inherent in our relationality; rather, it is attending to the question of responsibility that is important. As she notes: "Moral problems are observed and discussed from an attitude of caring, that is, with attentiveness, responsibility, responsiveness and the commitment to see issues from differing perspectives. The conclusion of this may not necessarily be a duty to care; it could also mean deciding not to provide care" (84). Whether or not we decide to take responsibility for that care will depend on a variety of situated, contextual factors such as resources, conflicting needs, or incompatible political commitments. The "attitude of caring" and the inherent responsibility to practise self-care forces those practices to move beyond the individual. This inclusion of responsibility could make the care that is practised in the techniques of self-care more robust and more clearly social.

If techniques of the self and care for the self are ways that we practise freedom, and if part of that care includes responsibility towards those to whom we are connected, then these techniques can lead to broader, more sustained patterns of resistance. If one is able to practise critical techniques of the self, then to do so ethically would include practising an attitude of caring for others. What I am describing here is similar to what Ouellette and Arcy (2015, 106) call care of the self as a "collaborative ethical project." They argue that the individual practices of care in which women (or, in their study, girls) engage can be linked in ways that create "networks of mutual care" (109) that, ultimately, can be spaces of resistance and action.

Several features of the work done by the alternative justice programs suggest that they incorporate this notion of responsibility into their work and thus link individual practices of self-care to collective forms of resistance. We see this focus on relationality and responsibility for care for the other in the focus the staff put on relationships. They recognize not only their relationship to the women with whom they work but also the variety of relationships within which the women are embedded. The inclusion of peer mentors demonstrates the link between caring for the self and caring for the other: women who have gone through the programs as participants come back into the programs as staff. The programs could cultivate and strengthen this caring attitude by making it an explicit part of their practices.

This is an area that is strongest in the Indigenous programs: the staff of these programs consistently linked the individual to the broader collective. One participant exemplified this in her interview with me, speaking about care of the self in this way:

> And I usually start with the most important relationship, which is the relationship with themselves. They need to know and understand and be comfortable in that relationship, first in order to have other relationships, and so I not only focus on the past relationship but we talk about all relationships.

She also talked about grounding the knowledge of the self in the past history of First Nations peoples in Canada. She then linked this to women going forward in a good way:

> Because usually people don't take time to think about themselves, they just do. And they're so busy in the world they just go on and on not realizing how things are affecting them. But, like, we talk about feelings and we talk about other people and we talk about the seven teachings, you know? And so something sparks inside of them because they know it's true. And so they stop for a minute and then they think about that. I think that really makes a difference.

Staff work with the women in order to meet their personal needs, and they consistently link those needs to the related care needs of their families and communities.

Resistance in the Informal/Formal Justice Complex

There is resistance present in the alternative justice programs studied here. But it is a fragile resistance and it requires constant, conscious reflection by practitioners so as to encourage and enable reflection in criminalized women. One way that this potential can be nurtured is to strengthen ties between agencies. Having staff from multiple agencies be able to come together and share and reflect could broaden and deepen the critical consciousness necessary to ensure that their work is resistant. This would be similar to the ways in which consciousness-raising groups operate. This practice is occasionally undertaken in Winnipeg. Onashowewin and Elizabeth Fry hosted a public event with speakers Kim Pate and Debbie Kilroy to discuss the challenges facing criminalized women. The discussion was critical of the criminal justice system – particularly corrections – but it also drew on broader critiques of colonialism and patriarchy. These types of events could strengthen, build, and disperse a resistant ethic of self within the justice complex.

The potential of this type of collaboration is constrained by the neoliberalization of the justice complex. It is only sporadically done at present, and participants spoke of very little connection between the agencies. Several acknowledged that part of the reason for the lack of collaboration was competition for funding dollars – despite the fact that most of the programs serve women with different needs or at different points in the justice process – although the programs do collaborate with agencies located outside of the justice complex. Participants spoke of their relationships with housing groups, social welfare organizations, a university, and other local community programs. While funding competition in the justice complex may limit the degree to which the alternative justice programs collaborate, it may push them to engage with non-justice agencies. These connections to non-justice agencies and to national organizations such as Elizabeth Fry, which is critical of the criminal justice system, potentially increases the possibility for self-conscious critique of the justice complex.

The potential for resistance is constrained by the programs' placement in the informal-formal justice complex. The process of "government at a distance" puts pressure on the programs to operate according to dominant mentalities. This placement of the programs and the ties they have to the formal justice system keep their work focused on criminal justice. The justice work that they do most closely resembles neoliberal strategies and mentalities of governance. It is when participants were talking about their justice work that the criminalized woman was most likely to be described as a neoliberal subject. For agencies that are not only justice agencies, such as the Native Women's Transition Centre, having a program in the justice complex may function to import neoliberal governance mentalities into their other programs. In this way, the justice complex not only constrains the potential for resistance but also may extend dominant mentalities into new spaces.

Resistance is also, however, enabled within the justice complex. Were it not for the justice relationships, the program staff may have no relationship with criminalized women at all. This connection to the criminal justice system provided the programs with resources, however meagre and rule-bound they may have been. Having some government funding may allow agencies to leverage other funds or give them some stability from which to fundraise and recruit volunteers. Official partnerships with the justice system also meant that agency staff, especially executive directors, might have regular contact with policy makers. By giving alternative justice programs the responsibility to govern women, neoliberal strategies also give them the ability to change what that governance looks like.

Resistance in this complex is unlikely to entail a massive overthrow of the informal-formal justice complex; rather, it will involve the reworking of these relations so as to understand the criminalized woman differently. And, as Sawicki (1991, 100) argues: "The fact that one cannot guarantee the outcome of such resistance is no argument against it. It is, instead, a reason to continue to be attentive to the limits of one's own discourses and practices." This analysis takes its inspiration from Foucault's (1988, 265) description of the work of the intellectual: "it is, through the analyses that he carries out in his own field, to question over and over again what is postulated as self-evident." I offer this analysis of resistance as a questioning of the critical criminological conclusion that community justice programs that engage in personal development strategies exhibit only normalizing, neoliberal governance. I also want to offer a caution to feminist criminology. In order to resist neoliberal governance, "feminists must critically assess our own methods, in Beatrice Webb's phrase, of 'governing and guiding' other women. Another way to say this is that feminism's will to empower other women must be intensely scrutinized. The problem for feminists is not whether to help other women but how; what form should helping take?" (Cruikshank 1999, 60). It is in this spirit that I focus on community alternatives. My analysis suggests that we, as feminists, should not be overly sanguine in our call for community alternatives. The potential for resistance to neoliberal governance is evident in the work these alternative justice programs do – but so, too, is their potential to contribute to that governance.

The main problem with alternative justice programs – their ability to not only support but also to strengthen the criminal justice system (Cohen 1985) – certainly exists in the work done by the agencies included in this study. In so far as their programs prop up the formal system, they severely constrain the potential for resistance. They carve out a small space for some difference, but, in so doing, they allow the overall response to criminalized women to be the dominant justice system response. Comack (1996, 140) identifies the irony of this for many of the incarcerated women whom she interviewed: "only after they were caught up in the criminal justice system did they receive access to resources they needed to begin resolving their troubles." In many ways the alternative justice programs studied here provide the material resources, critical reflection, and support women need; and, unlike the women in Comack's study, they provide them outside of a jail or prison. But a very serious constraint remains – namely, that women must be criminalized in order to gain access to these programs. Though the program staff constitute her as a marginalized woman, the reality is that, in most cases, marginalization is not enough to gain access to these programs. The woman must be criminalized.

Conclusion

Questions Raised

My analysis raises two primary questions, and neither is easily answered: First, should the women who are served by these agencies have to be criminalized in order to gain access to their alternative justice programs? Second, how is it that alternative justice work can function in concert with neoliberal strategies of governance? The first question follows from the concerns raised at the end of the last chapter. On the one hand, the seemingly obvious answer is no. The alternative aspects of the programs that I have identified are structured by social justice approaches to service work and, as such, are designed to be inclusive and based on women's needs. In addition to there being no necessary requirement to be involved with the justice system, there is, of course, the harms that come from that involvement. In many cases these programs are helping women avoid the harms of being incarcerated, but, even without spending time in carceral institutions, there are implications to being criminalized. There is the stigma of a criminal record, which can affect employment and volunteer activity. It can also affect women's ability to parent their children. The harm from criminalization is too great to justify it as an entry point to gaining access to services; indeed, many of the programs recognized this and noted that they would take referrals from outside of the justice system. Keeping alternative justice tied to the criminal justice system also maintains and reinforces neoliberal discourses and governance. There is also the concern that the incorporation of technologies of self-care, the alternative approach that the programs offer, cannot justify continued criminal justice intrusion into the lives of criminalized women. Answering the question in this way means that, no matter the differences between these programs and the justice system, we should be refocusing our efforts on removing women from the criminalization process altogether and addressing their needs absent any connection to the criminal justice system.

On the other hand, the risk remains that, by expanding this work to non-criminalized women, neoliberal mentalities and subjectivities are expanded into the lives of marginalized women more broadly. If the programs focused less on justice system referrals and more on marginalized women in the community, they could be contributing to the incorporation of other areas of social life into neoliberal governance. These programs could then be encouraging women to focus on taking responsibility for their social location and the need for individual change with respect to an even wider range of social problems. This is precisely the worry of scholars, such as Cohen (1985), Woolford and Ratner (2008), and Maglione (2014), who argue that alternative programs provide space for dominant discourses and mentalities to grow and expand into new arenas.

Of course, if those neoliberal tendencies can be limited, the potential exists for bringing the alternative aspects of the programs to more people. There may be the opportunity to bring feminist- and Indigenous-informed modes of governance into the lives of those who are on society's margins. Staff could offer practices of critical self-care and relationships of care and support to individuals before serious harm occurs. This, in turn, could strengthen the structural and social analysis to which the staff aspire. It could be an iterative process in which staff see broader connections between structures of inequality and thus encourage more critical reflection and collective action. The focus here would be on curtailing the neoliberal themes of the work staff perform. It may be that, if the programs severed ties with the criminal justice system, the neoliberal aspects of their work would diminish. It was in the justice work of the programs – the formal and informal justice work alike – that neoliberal ideas showed up most clearly.

If the programs broke contact with the justice system, this would mean no longer taking referrals from that system. It would mean not engaging in bail or legal order supervision. It would mean engaging in restorative justice only on the initiation of individuals, not through a legal process. Funding and employment through provincial and federal corrections would be terminated. The agencies would then be removed from the informal-formal justice complex. While I have argued it is this inclusion that keeps them tied to dominant mentalities, it is also what facilitates their work. It provides them with resources and with the connections to the women with whom they work and whom they support. Were the agencies to extricate themselves from this complex, they would need to find other ways to reach women. This is similar to what Woolford and Ratner (2008) call a retreatist model, the danger being that agencies who utilize it may become isolated and thus unable to offer alternatives to anyone.

A final worry about this course of action is what would happen to women who are criminalized. Just because alternative justice programs choose to focus on social justice rather than on criminal justice does not mean that the criminal justice system would follow suit. Indeed, as evidenced by the increasing number of women incarcerated in Canada, the justice system is engaged in precisely the opposite course of action. Were agencies such as the ones studied here to remove themselves from the justice complex, who would be serving criminalized women and meeting their needs? We might anticipate that this removal would contribute to the number of women in institutions as women would be forced to enter jail or prison to receive many of the services that are currently offered in the community. While the type of "alternative" offered by the programs may not be completely different from that offered by the criminal justice system, the programs do assist in what Hannah-Moffat (2001) argues is a necessary decentring of prisons as a justice response. Participants were not trying to reform prisons or jails as institutions: they were trying to provide services and justice to women outside of those institutions. On reflection, the question of continued criminal justice involvement is difficult and perhaps impossible to answer. The agencies are firmly enmeshed in the justice complex, and, while that may mean that they advance some neoliberal goals, my research found that they simultaneously pursue their own goals.

If we cannot easily detach alternative justice initiatives and their work from the justice complex, we must deal with the second primary question mentioned above: How is it that seemingly alternative justice work can function in concert with neoliberal strategies of governance? The programs here provide an example of a larger phenomenon identified by other scholars: the alignment of feminist and other social justice projects within neoliberalism. Goodkind (2009) argues there is a "union" of feminism and neoliberalism in the "commercialized feminism" she identifies as operative in social programs for young women. She argues that these programs offer strategies of individual change couched in the language of empowerment and personal pleasure; however, they ultimately work to create neoliberal subjects. Similarly, Allspach (2010) argues that criminalized women coming out of the criminal justice system remain in a web of social control, of which community agencies are a part. Scholars have identified similar trends in the movement to address violence against women. Bumiller (2008), for example, argues that feminist anti-violence movements have been entirely co-opted by neoliberal discourse. Bernstein (2010, 57), drawing on Bumiller's analysis, traces the development and deployment of carceral feminism, a strand of feminist thinking and activism that has arisen as "a result of feminists directly joining forces with a neoliberal project of social control." Bernstein analyzes carceral feminism in relation to human trafficking but connects it to campaigns against pornography, sex work, and broader violence against women campaigns. Instead of advancing broad-based systemic change and intersectional social justice, this strand of feminism supports tough criminal justice responses to crimes against women, conceptualizing "social justice as criminal justice" (58). Evident through these analyses are characterizations of the relationship between neoliberalism and feminism as all-encompassing: feminism has been appropriated and co-opted.

All these analyses have informed my own; however, there are notable differences throughout the data that have left me uneasy about adding my conclusions to this narrative about neoliberal co-optation. The focus on social justice, collective harm, and the resistant subject position of the marginalized woman were all too strong to allow me to conclude that these programs have been wholly appropriated by neoliberalism. Gotell's (2015) arguments resonate strongly with my analysis. She rebuts this characterization of neoliberal appropriation of feminism, arguing that the case is often overstated, that it uses a reductionist vision of the law and justice system as either oppressive or empowering. Instead, she reminds us that "feminists need to appreciate law as a site of discursive struggles, with contradictory implications" (61). Although she focuses specifically on legal reform, this point can be extended to the justice complex writ large.

I have struggled to make sense of the congruence of feminist and neoliberal strategies without reducing it to co-optation. The concept of alignment – the idea that, although the motivations and goals of various strategies may be vastly different, their interests can be the same – has assisted in clarifying this. Neoliberal strategies operate to specify particular limits to the array of options available to individuals, with the goal of proper conduct in that narrow field of action. Feminist strategies operate to open up the options available to people in order to achieve the goal of social justice. Yet both those very different goals can lead to strategies that emphasize education, training, work, and empowerment for individual criminalized women.

A specific example from my research is the personal advocacy work that staff do with individual criminalized women. They may assist a woman in gaining access to Employment and Income Assistance as a means of expanding her options. Their goal may be to enable this woman to have more ways of surviving and supporting her family and, thus, for her to have more possibilities of action in her life. This aligns with the interest that neoliberal governance has in citizens gaining access to things like EIA. Having an individual citizen navigate the bureaucracy and receive payment in lieu of, but in the course of securing, paid employment assists in the goal of having individuals act within limited parameters. Assisting the women in this way aligns with the interests of both feminist and neoliberal projects. It stops the woman from operating outside of the parameters of neoliberalism – for example, stealing what she needs or agitating in a collective way for entirely different economic arrangements. It also potentially allows the woman to have more options than she currently has. It aligns with feminist goals of keeping women safe (the state having responsibility for citizens) and ensuring a fairer distribution of resources. With very different motivations and goals, the same strategies make sense for both feminism and neoliberalism.

Using a governmentality perspective allows us to see how neoliberal and feminist or social justice projects align in a way that retains complexity and room for resistance. One question that arises is: How can feminism and other social justice movements engage productively within neoliberal relations of governance? Janet Newman (2013, 2012) uses data gathered from interviews with female activists to examine the ways in which feminism can work within contemporary conditions of governance. She finds, as do I, that feminist interests can align with and support neoliberal interests. The latter, however, can also be made to align with and support the former. Finally, feminist interests, discourse, and mentalities can be brought in to change neoliberal projects. In specific connection to the analyses throughout this book, Newman (2012, 44) analyzes the way that "'community' is traversed by multiple and often antagonistic political projects." She demonstrates not only how the community is constructed to be a new space of "government at a distance" but also how it is a space in which feminist and critical race activism occur. As governments looked to responsibilize communities and to construct community partnerships, they created spaces of neoliberal governance;

however, they also "offered new spaces of power that drew women into governance arrangements while also offering them resources that they could sometimes divert in their efforts to promote social justice" (46). That same potential exists in the alternative justice programs. Because staff constitute the criminalized woman as the marginalized woman, they make an effort to ameliorate her marginalization and to agitate for broader social justice.

Newman (2012, 2013) is not naively optimistic about the power of feminist and other oppositional movements. She notes that feminist successes are often small and unsustainable. Looking forward, she argues, "the spaces of power with which I have been concerned are shrinking, the borders tightening and material constraints couple with more coercive governance regimes make it more difficult for activists to find the time or resources for creative political work" (Newman 2013, 217). What Newman does, and what I have tried to do here, is show the moments of opposition – the potential for and the realization of resistance. This phenomenon needs to be studied further, with a focus, similar to Newman's (2012, 2013), on how feminists can use this alignment to further their own goals and resist those of neoliberal governance.

A more specific question flows from the preceding ones: How can programs such as the alternative justice programs examined here resist the tendency for dominant practices to be reproduced and/or align with those same dominant modes of governance in order to interrupt them? Postmodern and poststructuralist theorists are continually critiqued for being unwilling to provide alternatives. This may be the central problem feminists have in using these types of theories in the service of feminism. My reading of Foucault, Butler, and others in this tradition reveals that they do not completely disavow offering alternatives. They reject the possibility of "a way forward" that comes from a specific analysis and claims to be a universal solution. If we are to strive to move towards more just social relations, alternatives must be provided. To do so from a poststructural position means offering alternatives along with their critique, to argue that this alternative may be better but it will certainly not escape the thing to which it is an alternative, and the outcome may be worse than the current situation. Feminists often charge Foucault with lacking normative foundations and advocating a relativism that cannot contribute to a feminist project, pointing to his claim that "everything is dangerous." To appropriate his insights in a feminist manner we must use our own feminist standards to engage in the activism that he argues is necessitated by his work: "My point is not that everything is bad, but that everything is dangerous, which is not exactly the same thing as bad. If everything is dangerous, then we always have something to do. So my position leads not to apathy but to a hyper- and pessimistic activism" (Foucault 1994, 256).

I insist throughout this book that the work conducted by alternative justice programs is guided by the assumption that it can be dangerous; however, I would like to offer some suggestions that could increase that work's potential for resistance. It is in their non-justice-related work that alternative justice programs have the strongest potential for resistance. In their care, advocacy, and culture work, these programs constitute and respond to the marginalized woman. Doing more of this type of work can provide criminalized women with the support and services they need and enable the programs to engage in more resistant work. This will be further strengthened if the programs can keep their construction of the criminalized woman as a marginalized woman central to their understanding of women's needs. Staff need to be cognizant of when their analysis slips to the individual level, when they primarily construct the neoliberal subject and expect her to solve her own problems.

Working with criminalized women may also facilitate working with women outside of the criminal justice context. One of my main findings is how the work that the programs do, and the ways in which they think about the women with whom they work, transcends the criminological literature and the criminal justice field. The programs are part of the informal-formal justice complex, but they also have connections to and roles in child welfare, social assistance, medical intervention, and both government and activist fields. They have these connections because the women with whom they work are also involved in all of these other institutions. Strengthening these links could help staff not only retain their work with criminalized women but also enable them to work with women whom they encounter in these other fields.

Relatedly, community-based social justice agencies should consider recruiting staff and volunteers who do not come from a criminal justice background. In my research, only one of the fifteen participants came from a justice background; the remaining participants had diverse career and training backgrounds and had worked in a variety of front line services with men and women who required support. This may have assisted in the development of their critical analyses and their focus on social marginalization, as may be seen in Kate's comments:

> I came into social work late in life ... I wanted to work with women in domestic violence, so that was my focus working with women in domestic. I did that. I was doing counselling in a women's shelter. Then I moved back to Winnipeg, but ... I ended up here because it's still a women's organization. I've always wanted to work with women. And there's the same issues as the women I was dealing with in domestic violence, abuse, childhood sexual abuse, domestic abuse, poverty, addictions, dealings with social assistance, it's the same. It's all the same. Except the women here have the charges.

To assist in these efforts, it would be helpful for the programs to keep building partnerships with other community agencies outside of the justice field. At the same time, however, the programs I studied would be well served by strengthening their ties to each other. There is very little evidence of relationships between them at present. Programs should work to create space to come together and share their work and their analysis of the needs of criminalized women in Winnipeg. Developing inter-agency connections could provide greater support for individual staff members and could potentially lead to the development of more collective resistant strategies. Many of the staff with whom I spoke felt that the state should be providing a variety of supports and services to criminalized women. The agencies would be able to present a stronger case for this as a united group.

There is also a role here for critical scholars. We can assist alternative justice groups and groups engaged in social justice work to strengthen the work that they do and the resistance that they offer to dominant justice forms. I am advocating a particular role for researchers. It has become commonplace in recent years to speak of "public sociology" or "public criminology," a form of scholarly work wherein academics are encouraged to move beyond the academy and work with the public. The most commonly assumed form of that work, however, is the transmission of research results to an uniformed public (see, for example, Currie 2007). This form of public criminology is not necessarily consistent with the aims of feminism or other transformative perspectives (Nelund 2014), so it is not my intention to argue that we should be presenting our research to staff and other practitioners; rather, I suggest that we can facilitate the strengthening of the resistance work they are already doing. Woolford and Ratner (2008) suggest that, in order to disrupt dominant norms, alternative justice movements must "persevere as critical and reflexive agents" able and willing to imagine justice differently and make concrete interventions in the practice of that justice. As shown throughout this analysis, staff at the alternative justice programs are already doing this. They do not need researchers to tell them how to think about justice or what structural forces are affecting the women with whom they work. Staff are also, however, busy, and their focus is on serving women in a variety of ways. Rather than simply trying to bring our research to practitioners, critical scholars can assist by opening up space – physical, financial, and intellectual space – for staff to reflect on their work within a broad context. We can utilize our campus infrastructure and our research funding to create space for staff and other activists to hone their critical understandings of these issues. This means that we need to include our research and theoretical tools in a way that truly partners with and learns from community members rather than simply trying to teach them.

Questions Remaining

The bulk of this analysis has involved describing and theorizing the resistance present in alternative justice programs. That was not, however, my original objective. I did not initially think that I would find resistance to neoliberal mentalities in these programs. Though I had hoped that, because they worked with criminalized women, the programs would have more of a social justice orientation, my readings of both the feminist criminological literature and critical analyses of informal justice meant that I did not anticipate that this would be the case. So, although I hope that this analysis makes the resistance and unique efforts offered by the programs clear, I do not mean to suggest that they are either expected or commonplace. The most exciting finding, for me, is the degree to which the programs constitute the criminalized woman as the marginalized woman. This understanding is intersectional, and their assessment of social marginalization as an extremely pressing issue is important and supports feminist claims regarding the necessity of collective community action and engagement. The agencies' responses to the marginalized woman and their resistant actions flow from this constitution.

My expectations limited the degree to which I asked the participants questions related to resistance. I did not ask about activism, perhaps the most clearly resistant part of the work they do. My methodological choices further limited this opportunity. Conducting one-off interviews meant that I did not go back to my participants to explore the themes of marginalization, care, and resistance. And this, in turn, means that the analysis of what they do as resistance is my own: I did not ask them to reflect on what resistance means for them.

Another consequence of not expecting to find resistance is that I have spent the bulk of the analysis documenting and analyzing only one aspect of it: the governing discourse used by the staff. This is an important aspect of resistance, but it does not provide a complete picture. There are at least three other registers in which resistance must be analyzed in order to more fully understand its realization and impact.

One question that must be answered is: How do these discourses operate in practice? Do staff members practise what they discussed with me? Because of the simultaneous presence of social justice and neoliberal discourses, examining the actual work that the programs do could assist in clarifying the potential for resistance. Does one aspect of their discourse become more pronounced? One could imagine that this could be the case with either the resistant or the neoliberal aspects of their discourse. It could be that staff discussed with me a more aspirational interpretation of their work, one that may not, in practice, have the space to have an impact. The practices, or technologies, of governance are important and can, as governmentality scholars remind us, modify these mentalities. Observing those practices may show considerable change regarding the mentalities I have traced. The opposite could also be true. In their discussions with me, staff may have emphasized the responsibility of criminalized women to present a discourse they know is in alignment with their funders and official government partners. A third and more likely outcome is that, in examining the practices of alternative justice, nuance was given to the overlapping and conflicting discourses and subjectivities as neither take precedent yet both appear in and influence the alternative justice work in which staff engage. In any case, observational research of the alternative justice programs would provide a more complete picture of the ways in which power and resistance are deployed on the ground in alternative justice efforts.

A related, and crucial, question that must also be examined is: How do criminalized women respond to this interrelated form of governance? How do they take up or resist the subjectivities constructed in these programs? Future research should investigate how criminalized women experience, understand, and respond to alternative justice program discourses. What other understandings of themselves, justice, resistance, and power do criminalized women bring into these programs? Do they arrive with a strong sense of self that then comes into conflict with the subjectivities constructed by program staff? How do they take up, use, and/or resist the various versions of the criminalized woman that the programs construct? Future research could also examine the ways that criminalized women use the techniques of the self that the programs offer. Recall that Foucauldian feminists argue that we can only know if these practices are resistant by examining them. Future work must take as its object of study criminalized women's discourse.

Finally, the political and economic contexts in which these programs operate must be considered. In a critical read of the appropriateness of Foucault's work for feminist efforts, Soper (1993, 34) argues that it is not enough to identify resistant discourses because "what is critical to their advancement is the specific economic and political climate in which they are expressing their resistance, and this can be more or less favourable to their reception." The context affects not only their reception but also their articulation. This is linked to the question of whether these findings will have resonance in other cities across Canada. The political and economic context of Winnipeg, as well as the general criminal justice landscape, are similar to those found in major urban centres across Canada, so there is not much to suggest that these findings would be unique to Winnipeg. One notable feature of Winnipeg, which does make a mark on my analysis, is the innovative work being done by Indigenous peoples, particularly around justice. In addition to the programming described here there are initiatives such as the Bear Clan Patrol, a community group reactivated in 2015 "to provide personal security in the inner city in a non-threatening, non-violent and supportive way" (Bear Clan Patrol website at https://bearclanpatrol.org), and Drag the Red, a community initiative to search the Red River for the remains of missing Indigenous people. There is clear interest, and capacity, in Winnipeg's Indigenous community to develop alternative justice processes. This is not to say that this same critical community engagement is not happening across Canada. The events and protests that made up the national Idle No More movement (see Idle No More website at http://www.idlenomore.ca and Kino-nda-niimi Collective

[2014] for more on this movement) are indicators that this same capacity exists outside of Winnipeg.

A question that remains is how we, as feminist scholars, can ensure that our research and scholarship keep Indigenous women at the centre of our initiatives. As a feminist scholar, I understand that seeking social justice for women means seeking social justice for *all* women. This has been the spirit in which I have approached the study of feminist criminology, and it is a sentiment that was with me throughout the writing of this book. However, throughout this project, despite my intersectional intentions, I was continually reminded by participants, and had to remind myself, to include race and colonialism in my research. Class issues and, of course, gender issues were easily identified and incorporated into the research as these are inequalities that I have experienced. My privilege as a white settler Canadian was a constant barrier to fully developing the racialized aspect of my research. I say all of this because it is a fact of feminist criminology that Indigenous women will, and should, be at the centre of our scholarship and advocacy. Indigenous women are overwhelmingly the targets of institutional and personal violence. Our criminal justice system is disproportionately used in response to their behaviour. We must put our scholarship in the service of social justice for Indigenous women, and, in so doing, intersectional intentions are not enough. We must, for those who are non-Indigenous scholars, bring settler colonial theory, Indigenous feminism, and participatory methods into our research. I did not do this here, and though I have tried to be attentive to and highlight the unique experience of Indigenous women, this is the biggest limitation of my research.

One of the consistent findings in this book is that Indigenous agencies and staff are bringing some of the most critical alternative approaches to informal justice work. This should alert non-Indigenous feminists, and other critical scholars, to the fact that, while we should put our work at the service of Indigenous peoples, this can only be done in order to support the work Indigenous groups are already doing. The researcher's role is not to teach or to show Indigenous groups "the truth" but, rather, to make room for them to build and validate their own analyses. Our role is to ensure that we are using our platforms to ally with and amplify the voices of marginalized groups and to critique dominant systems, discourses, and cultures.

In conclusion, I return to the questions that motivated this research. What kinds of justice practices are available for criminalized women in the community? There are criminal justice practices that mirror the formal system, such as surveillance, responsibilization, education, and training. But there are also social justice practices that focus on supporting criminalized women. What kinds of work are done in these community spaces? Justice, care, advocacy, and culture work all take place with the overall project of governing criminalized women. What alternatives to the formal justice system do these programs offer to criminalized women? They offer an alternative that is both different from yet similar to that offered by the formal justice system. They offer a space in which the criminalized woman is encouraged to work on herself. In one sense, this is similar to the formal system and its focus on individuals remaking themselves into responsible citizens. In another sense, though, it is entirely different. The criminalized woman is encouraged to care for herself, to understand and be critical of the social context in which she finds herself. Indigenous women are encouraged to remake themselves in a way that is culturally grounded. It will be in identifying these moments and spaces of resistance, in coordinating and strengthening them, that we will be able to provide alternative justice and, ultimately, social justice to criminalized women.

Appendix: Theoretical and Methodological Considerations

A Feminist Poststructural Project

FEMINISM IS THE primary epistemological, theoretical, and political commitment of this book. As a feminist project, my research is motivated by an overarching commitment to end social injustice and oppression based on gender, race, class, sexuality, and other markers of difference. Although a diverse field, one generally unifying feature of feminist thought is a highly critical view of positivist claims of value or power-free knowledge (Flax 1990; Fraser and Nicholson 1990). Harding (1990, 87) argues that "objectivism places women and feminists firmly outside a tightly defended barricade within which is claimed to lie all there is of reason, rationality, scientific methods and truth." Feminists have argued that knowledge claims purported to be universal are based on the particular experience of privileged men (Haraway 1990; Nicholson 1990). This appendix outlines the ways in which I constructed the research project and the data upon which the book draws. Though I start from a poststructualist epistemology, one that sees all claims to knowledge as enactments of power relations, I do not hold with relativism. Throughout my work on this book I have struggled with a dilemma that Donna Haraway (1988, 579) outlines as follows:

> How to have simultaneously an account of radical historical contingency for all knowledge claims and knowing subjects, a

> critical practice for recognizing our own "semiotic technologies" for making meanings, and a no-nonsense commitment to faithful accounts of a "real" world.

The rest of this appendix describes some of the strategies and techniques I employed to collect and analyze data that were faithful to the ways in which the discourses I analyze exist in the justice complex.

Feminists have drawn on Foucault's notion of knowledge/power as an alternative way of thinking about epistemology. He, too, is critical of the idea that science or rationality can produce "Truth." Instead, Foucault argues that knowledge is always tied to power. The link he draws between knowledge and power goes beyond the idea that knowledge is power or that power can enable knowledge; rather, he argues "that power and knowledge directly imply one another; that there is no power relation without the correlative constitution of a field of knowledge, nor any knowledge that does not presuppose and constitute at the same time power relations" (Foucault 1977, 27). Foucault argues that knowledge and power always co-constitute and implicate one another.

Foucault's notion that all knowledge is implicated in power has been a particularly useful tool in helping feminists analyze the universalizing tendencies of feminism. If all knowledge is implicated in power, then there is an imperative to examine the ways in which feminist knowledge creates and reflects oppressive power relations. This is what Flax (1990, 48) suggests when she argues:

> We cannot simultaneously claim (1) that the mind, self and knowledge are socially constituted and that what we can know depends upon our social practice and contexts and (2) that feminist theory can uncover the truth of the whole once and for all.

Feminist scholars have used Foucauldian-inspired analyses to show that, when feminists speak of a universal "woman," they are denying the differing experiences, realities, and power relations that exist within that group based on other axes of difference, such as class, race, and sexuality (e.g., Butler 1995; Flax 1990).

Those working from a Foucauldian-inspired feminist position are not the only ones to critique essentialist notions of "woman." The unique contribution of poststructural feminism is the idea that we can never settle on a firm foundation of identity because "identity categories are never merely descriptive, but always normative, and as such exclusionary" (Butler 1995, 50). It is not simply a matter of adding other differences to our analyses but of always thinking about what our additions and definitions allow and disallow and how these are connected to power (Scott 1992). Foucault's concept of power/knowledge has, for me, meant that we can – and must – bring feminist knowledge and discourses into our critical analyses.

Judith Butler (1999) offered an extended and detailed theorization of gender according to this perspective. For Butler, gender is neither an intrinsic characteristic nor a cultural construct that follows from a pre-discursive sex; rather, gender is performative. It is not that gender causes people to become either masculine or feminine but that these identities cause gender, that is "that identity is performatively constituted by the very 'expressions' that are said to be its results" (33). Discourses, particularly the practices of compulsory heterosexuality, create the gendered identities of subjects. This is an unstable process, not a fixed event. Discourses must be repeated, and, in this repetition, there is room for failure and resistance. Butler's task is to "deconstruct the substantive appearance of gender into its constitutive acts and locate and account for those acts within the compulsory frames set by the various forces that police the social appearance of gender" (44). For poststructural feminists the goal is to destabilize discursive constructions of gender (Weedon 1997).

Research Design

The agencies under study were selected through a purposive and snowball sampling method. An internet search was conducted for Winnipeg agencies that provide service to women who have come into conflict with the law. The only sampling criteria for agency inclusion was that the agency be a non-profit social service organization that works with women. At each interview, I asked participants if they knew of other agencies doing this type of work. This process yielded six agencies: Onashowewin, Mediation Services, the Salvation Army, the Elizabeth Fry Society, the Native Women's Transition Centre, and New Directions, all of which run a variety of programs for criminalized women.

Onashowewin:
Restorative Justice Program

Mediation Services:
Restorative Action Centre

Salvation Army:
Positive Lifestyle Program
Prostitution Diversion Program

Elizabeth Fry Society:
Bail Verification and Supervision Program
Transitional housing units
Stoplifting
Women for change
Provincial reintegration worker

Native Women's Transition Centre:
Kihiw Iskewock Lodge

New Directions:
Transition, Education and Resources for Females (TERF)

The recruitment process was the same for all seven agencies. A letter was sent to the executive director (ED) of the agency. A follow-up phone call was made a week later, in which I both invited the ED to participate in an interview and requested the opportunity to recruit staff and volunteers. Once the initial contact was made with either the ED or program head at each agency, the recruitment process for staff varied. At two agencies I gave presentations to staff, circulated my contact information and recruitment letter, and asked anyone who was interested to get in touch with me. At one agency the ED introduced me to staff individually. These staff members gave me their contact information and I followed up with e-mail invitations to them to participate. At another agency the ED circulated my letter among staff, two participants responded, and I asked them to circulate my letter among volunteers. At one agency only one staff member was available, and at another agency the request to invite staff was denied by the ED because she felt they could offer no information beyond what she had already provided.

This study involved fifteen participants from six agencies. All the participants were agency staff. Though the number of participants is small, this is, in part, a reflection of the size of the agencies. The percentage of staff that participated ranges from 3.5 percent in one case to 80 percent in another. The smallest percentage was from the largest agency: New Directions. Most of this agency's work is non-justice related. So, although the percentage here is small, that is due to the fact that most staff do not work in the area in which I am interested. To the best of my knowledge, no Winnipeg agency that met the sampling criteria was excluded from the study.

Participants shared many demographic details. Only two of the participants were men. Though I did not ask them to do so, eleven of the fifteen participants identified as Indigenous. While several did not specify beyond saying they were Aboriginal or Native, some identified as Métis, Mohawk, or Inuit. Most had long careers in front-line service work, either in the agencies in which they were currently working or in other community agencies. Some came from social work backgrounds. A few became interested in justice-related work through their university studies. Only one participant identified as having formal justice system experience (she had spent several years as a correctional officer).

Each participant took part in a semi-structured, in-person interview. The interviews ranged from twenty-five minutes to just under two hours, with most being around an hour long. Each interview was structured around a set of predetermined questions designed to elicit descriptive data about the work being done, what the program does, the women with whom they work, and the relationship of the agency or programs to the criminal justice system. These questions served mainly as a guide, with the interviews sometimes going in unexpected directions at the lead of the participant. In most cases the first question – "Can you walk me through the process?" – was enough of a prompt for the participant to describe at length the work she or he did.

Participants were asked if they consented to the interview being audio-recorded and transcribed in full. All but two gave permission, and the two interviews that were not audio-recorded were documented with copious, sometimes verbatim, notes. An additional interview is not transcribed in full because of audio equipment failure. While I present no direct quotes from that interview, the notes I took reflect the themes generated from the rest of the data. This interview was the final one I conducted, so I knew that I was hearing things from this participant that I had heard from the others. Both summary and analytic notes were taken during all of the interviews and were later transcribed and treated as data. The audio-recordings were transcribed in full, and, in order to retain the voice of the participants, the interviews presented throughout this book are not significantly modified. Interviews have been edited to omit pauses and most interjections (um, like, so) unless they change or contribute to the meaning of the statements.

Throughout the presentation of the data I name the agencies and the programs they run. This was done in part because I wanted to give as much detail as possible about the programming offered by the agencies and did not feel I could do this while maintaining anonymity. It is my hope that nothing in this book will lead to negative consequences for the agencies. Participants were informed that the agency and programs would be named but that their identity would be kept confidential. Each participant was assigned a pseudonym, and this name accompanies most of the interviews. In some instances, no participant is identified. This is done mainly in cases in which the program or agency is named, as in "one participant from Onashowewin described her/his work as ..." In cases like this, I felt that presenting the pseudonym along with the name of the agency could potentially reveal the identity of the participant. A reader could link all of the statements made by that participant and identify where he or she works, thereby being able to make a reasonable guess as to her/his identity. In Winnipeg, the alternative justice community and non-profit community in general is small, so to fulfill my commitment to confidentiality the interviews are sometimes left unattributed.

As supplementary data, program documents were collected and analyzed. All of the content from the agencies' official websites were transcribed in full, and I conducted Google searches in order to find media- and government-related documents for each agency or program. I did not specifically ask participants for any documents, but in four cases they offered me material that ranged from program brochures not available online to intake forms, demographic statistics, and research reports carried out by the agencies. For one program I was also able to gain access to a large number of planning and partnership documents that had been collected for another research project.

The interviews form the core of my data. The documents I collected allowed me to better assess the saturation of the interview data. None of the information, themes, or identities that were present in the document data were absent from the interview data, while much of the interview data was present in the document data. In some cases, such as the case of the intake interview schedule, the documents allowed me to see in more detail aspects of the program about which the participants spoke. Wood and Kroger (2000) argue for the use of natural discourses in discourse analysis – discourses that do not occur at the researcher's behest. The document data in this study represent a more natural discourse of the programs under study, which mirrors the discourse produced through the interviews. This assists in confirming that, while the participants and I actively shaped the interviews, the transcripts reflect the discourses present in the agencies' work.

Data Quality

This book studies alternative justice discourse and the ways in which it draws on larger discourses. In gaining access to these discourses, I also participated in creating and perpetuating them. In a very concrete way these results cannot be generalized. The particular discourses outlined in this book were created by me and the participants, and while they draw on and replicate broader discourses, they were constructed during the interview process. That being said, there is reason to expect that the discourses drawn from these interviews bear a fair resemblance to those used by participants in their daily work. Discourses are not created anew with each individual; instead, we draw on dominant discourses. So, although the conversations between me and the participants are new, they were created by drawing on established understandings, knowledge, and ways of thinking and acting. I believe that the interviews reflect the discourses that staff bring to bear on their work. This belief rests on the criterion of saturation. Saturation is a key measure of data quality in qualitative research and refers to "collecting data until no new information is obtained" (Morse 1995, 147). The time between the interviews assisted in assuring that I reached saturation. The first interview took place in May 2013, the last in December of the same year. By the time I conducted the last three interviews in late November and early December, I had been organizing, coding, and analyzing the other interviews and could tell that nothing new was evident in the last three.

A variety of assumptions about my identity as researcher informed the context of the interviews. Based on my attendance at a large post-secondary institution and my appearance in the interviews (being well-dressed and arriving with a car and expensive recording equipment), participants seemed to assume I was middle class. Though I do come from a better-off background than many of the women with whom they work, it is still a working-class background. Although I have not struggled through the type of poverty that the participants described, their assumptions around my class position did not fit well with my experience. Regardless of my own unease with their assumptions, these assumptions led participants to make very clear the difficulties that arise for people living in poverty. As discussed in the introduction, my position as a white settler Canadian was apparent. I was at the time of the research, and clearly identified myself as, a student. I described my research as necessary to earn my doctorate, but I stressed that I wanted to learn from the participants. When this was combined with my relative youth, participants treated me very much as a student in need of being taught.

Ultimately, these identity markers and the difference between myself and my participants led to the interview context being primarily a teaching context. In assuming my ignorance of the realities of both their work and the lives of the women with whom they work, participants spent most of the interviews clearly outlining the basics of these issues. They did not, with the exceptions of three executive directors, spend any time theorizing their work. This led to the interviews being mainly descriptive. Indeed, they produced a wealth of descriptive data that I was able to analyze this for unarticulated assumptions and mentalities.

Though the participants may have exercised power in the interview context in the form of supplying and determining the data, I exercised considerable power in the subsequent analysis of that data and the writing of this book. I did give participants the option to review their transcripts and remove anything they felt may identify them or with which they were uncomfortable. Only five chose to review the transcripts and only two of those five made any changes, both of which involved interviews that had not been audio-recorded (and the changes made involved minor additions rather than deletions).

Method of Analysis

My poststructural position distinguishes my analytic strategy from other types of discourse analysis. Bacchi (2005, 199) distinguishes between two trajectories within discourse analysis research:

"a social psychological focus on patterns of speech (discourse analysis), and a political theoretical focus on the ways in which issues are given a particular meaning within a specific social setting (analysis of discourses)." My focus on power and inequality meant that conversation and discourse analysis were not sufficient tools. As I engaged in an analysis of discourse, my primary task was to identify the ways in which gender is constituted by participants, how that relies on larger discourses, and how that affects how governance strategies are discursively constituted. In order to do this I utilized some discourse analysis techniques, but my main task went beyond the linguistic construction of the texts under study to examine the ways in which they draw on and reinforce larger discourses of gender and governance.

This task could have been accomplished through critical discourse analysis (CDA). CDA is the analysis of the dialectical relationship between discourse and other elements of social practices, such as subjects, activities, and values (Fairclough 2003). This approach views discourse as a component of social practice. Fairclough identifies three ways that discourse works in social practice. First, discourse is an activity that is part of practice: in order to engage in certain practices, you need to use language in certain ways; second, practice is represented through discourse; and third, identities are partly constituted through representations in discourse. This critical perspective focuses on analyzing "relationships of dominance, discrimination, power and control as manifested in language" (Wodak 2001, 1).

Though there are similarities between the CDA approach and the poststructuralist approach, they come from fundamentally different ontological perspectives. The CDA approach focuses on how power is reproduced through discourse, while the poststructuralist approach focuses on how power relations and identities are constructed through discourse. In other words, those working in the poststructuralist tradition do not assume that a reality is reproduced in discourse. For their part, those working in the CDA tradition resist what they see as poststructuralism's reduction of social practice to discourse (Chouliaraki and Fairclough 1999).

This fundamental difference between CDA and poststructuralism means that, on a major theoretical point, this book is not a CDA.

That being said, poststructuralist literature is generally not methodologically robust. It is not sufficient for researchers who are looking for strategies on how to analyze data. One exception is Judith Baxter (2003, 2008, 2010), who offers both theoretical and methodological prescriptions for a feminist poststructuralist discourse analysis (FPDA). In contrasting it with CDA, she emphasizes what she calls the "anti-materialist tendency" of FPDA. Although she argues for FPDA as a distinct method, she does acknowledge that it complements CDA and can "be effective as a supplementary methodology" (Baxter 2008, 255). For this book I began from a poststructural theoretical position and situated CDA as a supplementary methodology, drawing upon it for several data analysis techniques.

Ramazanoglu and Holland (2002, 146) argue that, whatever the epistemological and methodological choices made by a researcher, "if feminist knowledge claims are to be well-founded, well-justified, and useful for social transformation, they must be able to stand up to criticism. Researchers should be clear about how their claims can be challenged and defended." It is in this spirit that I detail my methodological choices. It is my hope that this book will be especially useful for social transformation – that it may contribute to thinking about and doing justice differently.

Notes

Introduction

1 I use, and capitalize, "Indigenous" when discussing the original inhabitants of what is currently known as the sovereign nation-state of Canada. Although "Aboriginal" is a commonly used term – indeed, it was used by many participants – it has also been criticized for being assimilationist. Taiaiake Alfred (2005, 23), for example, argues that "this identity is a legal and social construction of the state, and it is disciplined by racialized violence and economic oppression to serve an agenda of silent surrender." The participants in this study use "Aboriginal" in a political context that values it as an official language. This is shifting, however, as the federal department responsible for the Indian Act has recently been renamed Indigenous and Northern Affairs.

2 These dates are approximate as it is difficult to identify exactly when and by what identifying events the Indian residential school system began and ended.

3 See appendix for a more detailed description of my research methodology.

4 When singular, these terms refer to the discursive subject position found in the literature or data; when plural, they refer to actual women with whom the programs may interact.

Chapter 1: Alternative Work

1 I use "social work" in its broadest possible sense. In Chapter 4, I argue that the type of activities I call "social work" are better thought of as "care work."

Chapter 2: Alternative Subjects

1 These, in the form of practices of self-care, are discussed further in the next chapter.

2 See McCorkel (2013) for a different correctional response in the American context.
3 See Crenshaw (1991); Hill-Collins (2000); Moraga and Anzaldua (1981).
4 The AJI released its final report in 1999. The inquiry was motivated by two particular cases in Manitoba: (1) the murder of Helen Betty Osborne, whose case took sixteen years to come to trial and resulted in the conviction of only one of the four men who were present at her death, and (2) the death of J.J. Harper, who "died following an encounter with a City of Winnipeg police officer. The following day the police department exonerated the officer involved" (AJIC 1999).
5 In the case of *R v. Gladue*, the Supreme Court of Canada ruled that judges must consider all sentencing options other than incarceration, with special attention to the circumstances of Aboriginal defendants. Gladue reports are submitted in bail and sentencing hearings. They detail the accused's community and the history of the individual, the goal being to place her/his behaviour in the social context of discrimination and colonization.

Chapter 3: Alternative Mentalities

1 One of the problems of trying to do this analysis as a settler is my inability to parse different Indigenous traditions, teachings, and ceremony. Emma LaRocque (2017, 139), in her critique of the ways in which gender oppression is reinscribed in calls for a return to tradition, notes that "what is culturally appropriate to a Blackfoot community may not be culturally appropriate to a Cree-Métis community, and so forth." Winnipeg is on the original lands of Anishinaabeg, Cree, Oji-Cree, Dakota, and Dene peoples, and is the homeland of the Métis. I have tried to draw out very broad themes that appear in the interviews but, in so doing, recognize the risk of universalizing.
2 One way in which settler colonialism has worked to "remove" Indigenous people is by constructing an "acceptable" Indigenous identity. The identity "Aboriginal" has been analyzed in this way (see Alfred 2005). Martel and Brassard (2008, 344) analyze the ways in which "the prison participates in the construction of an oversimplified, over-generalized vision of Aboriginal identity and imposes it on its Aboriginal populations." As a space in which criminal justice discourses are both replicated and refused, this same discursive practice may occur in alternative justice. My analysis suggests that something different and resistant is occurring with the programs' focus on culture work. In any case, this is a practice that further work on alternative justice should bear in mind.

Works Cited

Aboriginal Justice Implementation Commission (AJIC). 1999. *Report of the Aboriginal Justice Inquiry of Manitoba*. http://www.ajic.mb.ca/volume.html.

Alfred, Taiaiake. 2005. *Wasase: Indigenous Pathways of Action and Freedom*. Peterborough, ON: Broadview Press.

Alfred, Taiaiake, and Jeff Corntassel. 2005. "Being Indigenous: Resurgences against Contemporary Colonialism." *Government and Opposition* 40 (4): 597–614.

Allen, Amy. 2011. "Foucault and the Politics of Our Selves." *History of the Human Sciences* 24 (4): 43–59.

Allspach, Anke. 2010. "Landscapes of (Neo-)Liberal Control: The Transcarceral Spaces of Federally Sentenced Women in Canada." *Gender, Place and Culture: A Journal of Feminist Geography* 17 (6): 705–23.

Amigot, Patricia, and Margot Pujal. 2009. "On Power, Freedom, and Gender: A Fruitful Tension between Foucault and Feminism." *Theory and Psychology* 19 (5): 646–69.

Bacchi, Carol. 2005. "Discourse, Discourse Everywhere: Subject 'Agency' in Feminist Discourse Methodology." *Nordic Journal of Women's Studies* 13 (3): 198–209.

Baldry, Eileen. 2013. "Continuing Systemic Discrimination: Indigenous Australian Women Exiting Prison." In *Women Exiting Prison: Critical Essays on Gender, Post-Release, Support and Survival*, ed. Bree Carlton and Marie Segrave, 98–116. New York: Routledge.

Balfour, Gillian. 2006. "Re-imagining a Feminist Criminology." *Canadian Journal of Criminology and Criminal Justice* 48 (5): 735–52.

–. 2014. "Sentencing Aboriginal Women to Prison." In *Within the Confines: Women and the Law in Canada*, ed. Jennifer Kilty, 95–116. Toronto: Women's Press.

Balfour, Gillian, and Elizabeth Comack. 2014. "Introduction." In *Criminalizing Women: Gender and (In)Justice in Neo-Liberal Times,* 2nd ed., ed. Gillian Balfour and Elizabeth Comack, 1–10. Halifax: Fernwood.

Barnes, Marian. 2006. *Caring and Social Justice*. New York: Palgrave Macmillan.

Bartky, Susan. 1988. "Anorexia Nervosa: Pyschopathology as the Crystallization of Culture." In *Feminism and Foucault*, ed. Irene Diamond and Lee Quinby, 61–86. Boston: Northeastern University Press.

Baxter, Judith. 2003. *Positioning Gender in Discourse: A Feminist Methodology*. New York: Palgrave Macmillan.

–. 2008. "Feminist Post-Structuralist Discourse Analysis: A New Theoretical and Methodological Approach?" In *Gender and Language Research Methodologies,* ed. Kate Harrington, Lia Litosseliti, Helen Sauntson, and Jan Sunderland, 243–55. Basingstoke: Palgrave Macmillan.

–. 2010. *The Language of Female Leadership*. Basingstoke: Palgrave Macmillan.

Beck, Julie. 2006. "Recovering Selves." *Women and Therapy* 29 (3–4): 239–59.

Bernstein, Elizabeth. 2010. "Militarized Humanitarianism Meets Carceral Feminism: The Politics of Sex, Rights, and Freedom in Contemporary Antitrafficking Campaigns." *Signs: Journal of Women in Culture and Society* 36 (1): 45–71.

Bevir, Mark. 2010. "Rethinking Governmentality: Towards Genealogies of Governance." *European Journal of Social Theory* 13 (4): 423–41.

Blackstock, Cindy. 2007. "Residential Schools: Did They Really Close or Just Morph into Child Welfare?" *Indigenous Law Journal* 6 (1): 71–78.

–. 2011. "The Canadian Human Rights Tribunal on First Nations Child Welfare: Why if Canada Wins, Equality and Justice Lose." *Children and Youth Services Review* 33 (1): 187–94.

Blackstock, Cindy, Nico Trocmé, and Marlyn Bennett. 2004. "Child Maltreatment Investigations among Aboriginal and Non-Aboriginal Families in Canada." *Violence against Women* 10 (8): 901–16.

Boritch, Helen. 1997. *Fallen Women: Female Crime and Criminal Justice in Canada*. Toronto: Nelson Canada.

Bosworth, Mary. 2007. "Creating the Responsible Prisoner: Federal Admission and Orientation Packs." *Punishment and Society* 9 (1): 67–85.

Braithwaite John. 1996. "Restorative Justice and a Better Future." *Dalhousie Review* 76 (1): 9–31.

Brandon, Josh, and Evelyn Peters. 2014. *Moving to the City: Housing and Aboriginal Migration to Winnipeg*. Winnipeg: Canadian Centre for Policy Alternatives Manitoba Office.

BUILD (Building Urban Industries for Local Development). 2014. http://buildinc.ca/.

Bumiller, Kristin. 2008. *In an Abusive State: How Neoliberalism Appropriated the Feminist Movement against Sexual Violence*. Durham, NC: Duke University Press.

Burchell, Graham. 1996. "Liberal Government and Techniques of the Self." In *Foucault and Political Reason: Liberalism, Neo-Liberalism and Rationalities of Government*, ed. Andrew Barry, Thomas Osborne, and Nikolas Rose, 19–36. Chicago: University of Chicago Press.

Butler, Judith. 1995. "Contingent Foundations." In *Feminist Contentions: A Philosophical Exchange*, ed. Linda Nicholson, 35–58. New York: Routledge.

–. 1999. *Gender Trouble: Feminism and the Subversion of Identity*. New York: Routledge.

Carlen, Pat. 2002. "New Discourses of Justification and Reform for Women's Imprisonment in England." In *Women and Punishment: The Struggle for Justice*, ed. Pat Carlen, 220–36. Portland: Willan Publishing.

Chartrand, Vicki. 2015. "Landscapes of Violence: Women and Canadian Prisons." Champ Pénal/Penal Field, 12. Retrieved from https://champpenal.revues.org/9158.

Chouliaraki, Lilie, and Norman Fairclough. 1999. *Discourse in Late Modernity: Rethinking Critical Discourse Analysis*. Edinburgh: Edinburgh University Press.

Christie, Nils. 1977. "Conflicts as Property." *British Journal of Criminology* 17 (1): 1–15.

Cohen, Stanley. 1985. *Visions of Social Control*. Cambridge: Polity Press.

Comack, Elizabeth. 1996. *Women in Trouble*. Halifax: Fernwood.

–. 2006. "The Feminist Engagement with Criminology." In *Criminalizing Women: Gender and (In)Justice in Neo-Liberal Times*, ed. Gillian Balfour and Elizabeth Comack, 12–46. Halifax: Fernwood.

–. 2014. "Part II Introduction." In *Criminalizing Women: Gender and (In)Justice in Neo-Liberal Times*, 2nd ed., ed. Gillian Balfour and Elizabeth Comack, 48–72. Halifax: Fernwood.

–. 2018. *Coming Back to Jail: Women, Trauma, and Criminalization*. Halifax: Fernwood.

Comack, Elizabeth, and Salena Brickey. 2007. "Constituting the Violence of Criminalized Women." *Canadian Journal of Criminology and Criminal Justice* 49 (1): 1–36.

Corcoran, Mary. 2011. "Dilemmas of Institutionalization in the Penal Voluntary Sector." *Critical Social Policy* 31 (1): 30–52.

Crawford, Adam. 1997. *The Local Governance of Crime: Appeals to Community and Partnerships*. Oxford: Oxford University Press.

Crenshaw, Kimberlé. 1991. "Mapping the Margins: Intersectionality, Identity Politics, and Violence against Women of Colour." *Stanford Law Review* 43 (6): 1241–99.

Cruikshank, Barbara. 1996. "Revolutions Within: Self-Government and Self-Esteem." In *Foucault and Political Reason: Liberalism, Neo-liberalism and Rationalities of Government*, ed. Andrew Barry, Thomas Osborne, and Nikolas Rose, 231–52. Chicago: University of Chicago Press.

–. 1999. *The Will to Empower: Democratic Citizens and Other Subjects*. Ithaca: Cornell University Press.

Currie, Elliott. 2007. "Against Marginality: Arguments for a Public Criminology." *Theoretical Criminology* 11 (2): 175–90.

Daly, Kathleen. 2002. "Restorative Justice: The Real Story." *Punishment and Society* 4 (1): 55–79.

Dean, Mitchell. 1999. *Governmentality*. London: Sage.

Dej, Erin. 2016. "Psychocentrism and Homelessness: The Pathologization/Responsibilization Paradox." *Studies in Social Justice* 10 (1): 117–35.

Diamond, Irene, and Lee Quinby. 1988. *American Feminism and the Language of Control*. In *Feminism and Foucault: Reflections on Resistance*, ed. Irene Diamond and Lee Quinby, 193–206. Boston: Northeastern University Press.

Duits, Linda, and Liesbet van Zoonen. 2006. "Headscarves and Porno-Chic: Disciplining Girls' Bodies in the European Multicultural Society." *European Journal of Women's Studies* 13 (2): 103–17.

–. 2007. "Who's Afraid of Female Agency? A Rejoinder to Gill." *European Journal of Women's Studies* 14 (2): 161–70.

Elliott, Elizabeth. 2011. *Security with Care: Restorative Justice and Healthy Societies*. Halifax: Fernwood.

Evans, Adrienne, Sarah Riley, and Avi Shankar. 2010. "Technologies of Sexiness: Theorizing Women's Engagement in the Sexualization of Culture." *Feminism and Psychology* 20 (1): 114–31.

Fairclough, Norman. 2003. *Analysing Discourse: Textual Analysis for Social Research*. New York: Routledge.

Faith, Karlene. 1993. *Unruly Women: The Politics of Confinement and Resistance*. Vancouver: Press Gang.

Feenan, Dermot. 2002. "Re-introducing Informal Criminal Justice." In *Informal Criminal Justice,* ed. Dermot Feenan. Ashgate: Dartmouth Publishing.

Flax, Jane. 1990. "Postmodernism and Gender Relations in Feminist Theory." In *Feminism/Postmodernism*, ed. Linda Nicholson, 39–62. London: Routledge.

–. 1992. "The End of Innocence." In *Feminists Theorize the Political*, ed. Judith Butler and Joan Scott, 445–63. New York: Routledge.

Fontaine, Nahanni. 2014. "Surviving Colonization: Anishinaabe Ikwe Street Gang Participation." In *Criminalizing Women: Gender and (In)Justice in Neo-Liberal Times*, 2nd ed., ed. Gillian Balfour and Elizabeth Comack, 113–29. Halifax: Fernwood.

Foucault, Michel. 1977. *Discipline and Punish: The Birth of the Prison*. New York: Pantheon Books.
–. 1978. *The History of Sexuality. Vol. 1: An Introduction*. New York: Vintage Books.
–. 1980. "Two Lectures." In *Power/Knowledge: Selected Interviews and Other Writings*, ed. Colin Gordon, 78–108. New York: Pantheon Books.
–. 1988. "Critical Theory/Intellectual History." In *Michel Foucault*, ed. L. Kritzman, 17–46. London: Routledge.
–. 1991. "Governmentality." In *The Foucault Effect: Studies in Governmentality*, ed. Graham Burchell, Colin Gordon, and Peter Miller, 87–104. Chicago: University of Chicago Press.
–. 1994. *Ethics: Subjectivity and Truth – Essential Works of Foucault, 1954–1984*, vol. 1, ed. Paul Rabinow. New York: New Press.
–. 2008. *The Birth of Biopolitics: Lectures at the Collège de France, 1978–1979*, trans. Graham Burchell. New York: Picador.
Fraser, Nancy. 1989. *Unruly Practices: Power, Discourse, and Gender in Contemporary Social Theory*. Minneapolis: University of Minnesota Press.
–. 1995. "False Antithesis." In *Feminist Contentions: A Philosophical Exchange*, ed. Linda Nicholson, 59–74. New York: Routledge.
Fraser, Nancy, and Linda Nicholson. 1990. "Social Criticism without Philosophy: An Encounter between Feminism and Postmodernism." In *Feminism/Postmodernism*, ed. Linda Nicholson, 19–38. London: Routledge.
Garland, David. 1996. "The Limits of the Sovereign State: Strategies of Crime Control in Contemporary Society." *British Journal of Criminology* 36 (4): 445–71.
–. 1997. "'Governmentality' and the Problem of Crime: Foucault, Criminology, Sociology." *Theoretical Criminology* 1 (2): 173–214.
Gill, Rosalind. 2007. "Critical Respect: The Difficulties and Dilemmas of Agency and 'Choice' for Feminism: A Reply to Duits and van Zoonen." *European Journal of Women's Studies* 14 (1): 69–80.
Gilligan, Carol. 1982. *In a Different Voice: Psychological Theory and Women's Development*. Cambridge: Harvard University Press.
Goodkind, Sara. 2009. "'You Can Be Anything You Want, But You Have to Believe It': Commercialized Feminism in Gender-Specific Programs for Girls." *Signs* 34 (2): 397–422.
Gotell, Lise. 2015. "Reassessing the Place of Criminal Law Reform in the Struggle against Sexual Violence." In *Rape Justice: Beyond the Criminal Law*, ed. Anastasia Powell, Nicola Henry, and Asher Flynn, 53–71. Hampshire: Palgrave Macmillan.
Grimshaw, Jean. 1993. "Practices of Freedom." In *Up Against Foucault: Explorations of Some Tensions between Foucault and Feminism*, ed. Caroline Ramazanoglu, 51–72. London: Routledge.

Haber, Honi. 1996. "Foucault Pumped: Body Politics and the Muscled Woman." In *Feminist Interpretations of Michel Foucault*, ed. Susan Hekman, 137–56. University Park: Pennsylvania State University Press.

Haney, Lynne. 1996. "Homeboys, Babies, Men in Suits: The State and the Reproduction of Male Dominance." *American Sociological Review* 61 (5): 759–78.

–. 2010. *Offending Women: Power, Punishment, and the Regulation of Desire*. Berkeley: University of California Press.

Hannah-Moffat, Kelly. 2000. "Re-forming the Prison: Rethinking Our Ideal." In *An Ideal Prison? Critical Essays on Women's Imprisonment in Canada*, ed. Kelly Hannah-Moffat and Margaret Shaw, 30–40. Halifax: Fernwood.

–. 2001. *Punishment in Disguise: Penal Governance and Federal Imprisonment of Women in Canada*. Toronto: University of Toronto Press.

–. 2004. "Losing Ground: Gendered Knowledges, Parole Risk, and Responsibility." *Social Politics: International Studies in Gender, State and Society* 11 (3): 363–85.

–. 2005. "Criminogenic Needs and the Transformative Risk Subject." *Punishment and Society* 7 (1): 29–51.

–. 2010. "Sacrosanct or Flawed: Risk, Accountability and Gender-Responsive Penal Politics." *Current Issues in Criminal Justice* 22 (2): 193–215.

Hannah-Moffat, Kelly, and Margaret Shaw. 2001. "Introduction: Prisons for Women – Theory, Reform, Ideals." In *An Ideal Prison? Critical Essays on Women's Imprisonment in Canada*, ed. Kelly Hannah-Moffat and Margaret Shaw, 11–27. Halifax: Fernwood.

Hannah-Moffat, Kelly, and Amy Klassen. 2015. "Normalizing Expectations: Solitary Confinement and the Micro-Politics of Risk/Need in Canada." In *Extreme Punishment: Comparative Studies in Detention, Incarceration and Solitary Confinement*, ed. Keramet Reiter and Alexa Koenig, 135–55. New York: Palgrave Macmillan.

Haraway, Donna. 1988. "Situated Knowledges: The Science Question in Feminism and the Privilege of Partial Perspective." *Feminist Studies* 14 (3): 575–99.

–. 1990. "A Manifesto for Cyborgs: Science, Technology, and Socialist Feminism in the 1980s." In *Feminism/Postmodernism*, ed. Linda Nicholson, 190–233. London: Routledge.

Harding, Sandra. 1990. "Feminism, Science, and the Anti-Enlightenment Critiques." In *Feminism/Postmodernism*, ed. Linda Nicholson, 83–106. London: Routledge.

Harrington, Carol. 2012. "Prostitution Policy Models and Feminist Knowledge Politics in New Zealand and Sweden." *Sexuality Research and Social Policy* 9 (4): 337–49.

Harstock, Nancy. 1990. "Foucault on Power: A Theory for Women?" In *Feminism/Postmodernism*, ed. Linda Nicholson, 190–233. London: Routledge.

Hayman, Stephanie. 2006. *Imprisoning Our Sisters: The New Federal Women's Prisons in Canada*. Montreal and Kingston: McGill-Queen's University Press.

Hesse-Biber, Sharlene. 2014. "Feminist Approaches to In-Depth Interviewing." In *Feminist Research Practice: A Primer*, 2nd ed., ed. Sharlene Hesse-Biber, 182–232. Los Angeles: Sage.

Heyes, Cressida. 2007. *Self-Transformations: Foucault, Ethics, and Normalized Bodies*. Oxford: Oxford University Press.

Hill-Collins, Patricia. 2000. *Black Feminist Thought: Knowledge, Consciousness, and the Politics of Empowerment*, 2nd ed. New York: Routledge.

Hughes, Ted. 2013. *The Legacy of Phoenix Sinclair: Achieving the Best for All Our Children*. http://www.phoenixsinclairinquiry.ca/rulings/ps_volume1.pdf.

Johnson, Holly, and Karen Rodgers. 1993. "A Statistical Overview of Women and Crime in Canada." In *In Conflict with the Law: Women and the Canadian Justice System*, ed. Ellen Adelberg and Claudia Currie, 95–116. Vancouver: Press Gang.

Kemshall, Hazel. 2004. "Risk, Dangerousness, and Female Offenders." In *Women Who Offend*, ed. Gill McIvor, 209–26. London: Jessica Kingsley Publishers.

Kilroy, Debbie, Phoebe Barton, Suzi Quixley, Amanda George, and Emma Russel. 2013. "Decentring the Prison: Abolitionist Approaches to Working with Criminalized Women." In *Women Exiting Prison: Critical Essays on Gender, Post-Release, Support and Survival*, ed. Bree Carlton and Marie Segrave, 156–80. New York: Routledge.

Kilty, Jennifer. 2006. "Under the Barred Umbrella: Is There Room for a Woman Centered Self-Injury Policy in Canadian Corrections?" *Criminology and Public Policy* 5 (1): 161–82.

–. 2012. "It's Like They Don't Want You to Get Better: Psy Control of Women in the Carceral Context." *Feminism and Psychology* 22 (2): 162–82.

–. 2014. "Examining the 'Psy-Carceral Complex' in the Death of Ashley Smith." In *Criminalizing Women: Gender and (In)Justice in Neo-Liberal Times*, 2nd ed., ed. Gillian Balfour and Elizabeth Comack, 236–52. Halifax: Fernwood.

Kilty, Jennifer, and Erin Dej. 2012. "Anchoring amongst the Waves: Discursive Constructions of Motherhood and Addiction." *Qualitative Sociology Review* 8 (3): 6–23.

Kino-nda-niimi Collective. 2014. *The Winter We Danced: Voices from the Past, the Future, and the Idle No More Movement*. Winnipeg: ARP Books.

Kong, Rebecca, and Kathy AuCoin. 2008. *Female Offenders in Canada*. Ottawa: Statistics Canada. https://www150.statcan.gc.ca/n1/en/catalogue/85-002-X200800110509.

LaCombe, Dany. 2008. "Consumed with Sex: The Treatment of Sex Offenders in Risk Society." *British Journal of Criminology* 48: 55–74.

Landertinger, Laura. 2015. "Settler Colonialism and Carceral Control of Indigenous Mothers and Their Children: Child Welfare and the Prison System." In *Criminalized Mothers, Criminalizing Mothering*, ed. Joanne Minaker and Bryan Hogeveen, 59–87. Bradford: Demeter Press.

Larner, Wendy. 2000. "Neoliberalism: Policy, Ideology, Governmentality." *Studies in Political Economy* 63 (1): 5–25.

LaRocque, Emma. 2017. "Métis and Feminist: Contemplations on Feminism, Human Rights, Culture and Decolonization." In *Making Space for Indigenous Feminism,* 2nd ed., ed. Joyce Green, 122–45. Halifax: Fernwood.

Leitner, Helga, Eric Sheppard, Kristin Sziarto, and Anant Maringanti. 2007. "Contesting Urban Futures: Decentring Neoliberalism." In *Contesting Neoliberalism: Urban Frontiers*, ed. Helga Leitner, Jamie Peck, and Eric Sheppard, 1–25. New York: Guilford Press.

Llewellyn, Jennifer. 2012. "Restorative Justice: Thinking Relationally about Justice." In *Being Relational: Reflections on Relational Theory and Health Law and Policy*, ed. Jocelyn Downie and Jennifer Llewellyn, 89–108. Vancouver: UBC Press.

Lloyd, Moya. 1996. "A Feminist Mapping of Foucauldian Politics." In *Feminist Interpretations of Michel Foucault*, ed. Susan Hekman, 241–64. University Park: Pennsylvania State University Press.

Loucks, Nancy. 2004. "Women in Prison." In *Women Who Offend*, ed. Gill McIvor, 142–58. London: Jessica Kingsley Publishers.

Maclean, Kate. 2013. "Gender, Risk and Micro-financial Subjectivities." *Antipode* 45 (2): 455–73.

Macleod, Catriona, and Kevin Durrheim. 2002. "Foucauldian Feminism: The Implications of Governmentality." *Journal for the Theory of Social Behaviour* 32 (1): 41–60.

Maglione, Giuseppe. 2014. "Discursive Fields and Subject Positions: Becoming 'Victim,' 'Offender' and 'Community' in Restorative Justice." *Restorative Justice* 2 (3): 327–48.

Mahony, Tina. 2011. *Women and the Criminal Justice System*. Ottawa: Statistics Canada. https://www150.statcan.gc.ca/n1/pub/89-503-x/2015001/article/14785-eng.pdf.

Maidment, MaDonna. 2006a. *Doing Time on the Outside: Deconstructing the Benevolent Community*. Toronto: University of Toronto Press.

–. 2006b. "We're Not All That Criminal." *Women and Therapy* 29 (3–4): 35–56.

Marshall, Tony. 1999. *Restorative Justice: An Overview*. London: Home Office Research Development and Statistics Directorate.

Martel, Joane. 2000. "Women in the 'Hole': The Unquestioned Practice of Segregation." In *An Ideal Prison? Critical Essays on Women's Imprisonment in Canada*, ed. Kelly Hannah-Moffat and Margaret Shaw, 128–35. Halifax: Fernwood.

Martel, Joane, and Renée Brassard. 2008. "Painting the Prison 'Red': Constructing and Experiencing Aboriginal Identities in Prison." *British Journal of Social Work* 38: 340–61.

Martin, Biddy. 1988. "Feminism, Criticism and Foucault." In *Feminism and Foucault*, ed. Irene Diamond and Lee Quinby, 3–19. Boston: Northeastern University Press.

Maslow, Abraham. 1943. "A Theory of Human Motivation." *Psychological Review* 50: 370–96.

Maurutto, Paula, and Kelly Hannah-Moffat. 2006. "Assembling Risk and the Restructuring of Penal Control." *British Journal of Criminology* 46 (3): 438–54.

McCorkel, Jill. 2003. "Embodied Surveillance and the Gendering of Punishment." *Journal of Contemporary Ethnography* 32 (1): 41–76.

–. 2013. *Breaking Women: Gender, Race, and the New Politics of Imprisonment*. New York: New York University Press.

McKim, Allison. 2008. "'Getting Gut-Level': Punishment, Gender and Therapeutic Governance." *Gender and Society* 22: 303–23.

McLaren, Margaret. 2002. *Feminism, Foucault, and Embodied Subjectivity*. Albany: State University of New York Press.

–. 2004. "Foucault and Feminism: Power, Resistance, Freedom." In *Feminism and the Final Foucault*, ed. Dianna Taylor and Karen Vintges, 214–34. Chicago: University of Illinois Press.

McNay, Lois. 1992. *Feminism and Foucault*. Cambridge: Polity Press.

McWhorter, Ladelle. 1999. *Bodies and Pleasures: Foucault and the Politics of Sexual Normalization*. Bloomington: Indiana University Press.

–. 2004. "Practicing Practicing." In *Feminism and the Final Foucault*, ed. Dianna Taylor and Karen Vintges, 143–62. Chicago: University of Illinois Press.

–. 2013. "Post-Liberation Feminism and Practices of Freedom." *Foucault Studies* 16: 54–73.

Miller, Reuben. 2014. "Devolving the Carceral State: Race, Prisoner Reentry, and the Micro-Politics of Urban Poverty Management." *Punishment and Society* 16 (3): 305–35.

Minaker, Joanne. 2014. "Sluts and Slags: The Censuring of the Erring Female." In *Criminalizing Women: Gender and (In)justice in Neo-Liberal Times*, ed. Gillian Balfour and Elizabeth Comack, 73–87. Halifax: Fernwood.

Minaker, Joanne, and Bryan Hogeveen. 2015. "From Criminalizing Mothering to Criminalized Mothers: An Introduction." In *Criminalized Mothers, Criminalizing Mothering*, ed. Joanne Minaker and Bryan Hogeveen, 1–26. Bradford: Demeter Press.

Minaker, Joanne, and Bryan Hogeveen, eds. 2015. *Criminalized Mothers, Criminalizing Mothering*. Bradford: Demeter Press.

Monchalin, Lisa. 2017. *The Colonial Problem: An Indigenous Perspective on Crime and Injustice in Canada*. Toronto: University of Toronto Press.

Monture-Angus, Patricia. 1995. *Thunder in My Soul: A Mohawk Woman Speaks*. Halifax: Fernwood.

–. 1999. "Women and Risk: Aboriginal Women, Colonialism and Correctional Practice." *Canadian Women Studies* 19 (2): 24–29.

Moraga, Cherrie, and Gloria Anzaldua, eds. 1981. *This Bridge Called My Back: Writings by Radical Women of Color*. Watertown: Persephone Press.

Morse, Janice. 1995. "The Significance of Saturation." *Qualitative Health Research* 5: 147.

Native Women's Association of Canada (NWAC). 2010. *What Their Stories Tell Us: Research Findings from the Sisters in Spirit Initiative*. http://www.nwac.ca/wp-content/uploads/2015/05/2010_What_Their_Stories_Tell_Us_Research_Findings_SIS_Initiative.pdf.

Nelund, Amanda. 2014. "Troubling Publics: A Feminist Analysis of Public Criminology." *Radical Criminology* 4: 67–84.

Newman, Janet. 2012. *Working the Spaces of Power: Activism, Neoliberalism and Gendered Labour*. London: Bloomsbury Academic.

–. 2013. "Spaces of Power: Feminism, Neoliberalism, and Gendered Labor." *Social Politics* 20 (2): 200–21.

Nicholson, Linda. 1990. "Introduction." In *Feminism/Postmodernism*, ed. Linda Nicholson, 1–18. London: Routledge.

Office of the Correctional Investigator. 2014. Annual Report, 2013–2014. http://www.oci-bec.gc.ca/index-eng.aspx.

–. 2015. Annual Report, 2014–2015. http://www.oci-bec.gc.ca/index-eng.aspx.

–. 2016. Annual Report, 2015–2016. http://www.oci-bec.gc.ca/index-eng.aspx.

–. 2017. Annual Report, 2016–2017. https://www.oci-bec.gc.ca/cnt/rpt/annrpt/annrpt20162017-eng.aspx.

O'Grady, Helen. 2004. "An Ethics of the Self." In *Feminism and the Final Foucault*, ed. Dianna Taylor and Karen Vintges, 91–117. Chicago: University of Illinois Press.

Oksala, Johanna. 2005. *Foucault on Freedom*. Cambridge: Cambridge University Press.

–. 2013. "Feminism and Neoliberal Governmentality." *Foucault Studies* 16: 32–53.

O'Malley, Pat. 1999. "Consuming Risks: Harm Minimization and the Government of 'Drug Users.'" In *Governable Places: Readings on Governmentality and Crime Control*, ed. Russell Smandych, 191–214. Brookfield, VT: Ashgate.

Open Letter to Chief Commissioner Marion Buller. 2017. https://nbmediacoop.org/2017/05/16/open-letter-to-chief-commissioner-marion-buller-on-the-national-inquiry-on-missing-and-murdered-indigenous-women-and-girls. Last viewed 19 May 2020.

Ouellette, Laurie, and Jacquelyn Arcy. 2015. "'Live Through This': Feminist Care of the Self 2.0." *Frame* 28 (1): 95–114.

Pavlich, George. 2005. *Governing Paradoxes of Restorative Justice*. London: Glasshouse Press.

–. 2001 "The Force of Community." In *Restorative Justice and Civil Society*, ed. Heather Strang and John Braithwaite, 56–68. Cambridge: Cambridge University Press.

Perreault, Samuel. 2015. *Criminal Victimization in Canada 2014*. Canadian Centre for Justice Statistics.

Pollack, Shoshana. 2000. "Reconceptualizing Women's Agency and Empowerment: Challenges to Self-Esteem Discourse and Women's Lawbreaking." *Women and Criminal Justice* 12 (1): 75–89.

–. 2006. "Therapeutic Programming as a Regulatory Practice in Women's Prisons." In *Criminalizing Women: Gender and (In)Justice in Neoliberal Times*, ed. Gillian Balfour and Elizabeth Comack, 236–49. Halifax: Fernwood.

–. 2007. "'I'm Just Not Good in Relationships': Victimization Discourses and the Gendered Regulation of Criminalized Woman." *Feminist Criminology* 2 (2): 158–74.

–. 2009. "'Circuits of Exclusion': Criminalized Women's Negotiation of Community." *Canadian Journal of Community Mental Health* 28 (1): 83–95.

–. 2013. "An Imprisoning Gaze: Practices of Gendered, Racialized and Epistemic Violence." *International Review of Victimology* 19 (1): 103–14.

Pollack, Shoshana, and Amy Rossiter. 2010. "Neoliberalism and the Entrepreneurial Subject: Implications for Feminism and Social Work." *Canadian Social Work Review/Revue canadienne de service social* 27 (2): 155–69.

Prochaska, James, Carol DiClemente, and John Norcross. 1992. "In Search of How People Change: Applications to Addictive Behaviors." *American Psychologist* 47 (9): 1102–14.

Public Safety Canada. 2017. *Corrections and Conditional Release Statistical Overview*. Ottawa: Public Works and Government Services Canada.

Raby, Rebecca. 2005. "What Is Resistance?" *Journal of Youth Studies* 8 (2): 151–71.

Ramazanoglu, Caroline. 1993. "Introduction." In *Up Against Foucault: Explorations of Some Tensions between Foucault and Feminism*, ed. Caroline Ramazanoglu, 1–28. London: Routledge.

Ramazanoglu, Caroline, and Janet Holland. 2002. *Feminist Methodology: Challenges and Choices*. London: Sage.

Ranasinghe, Prashan. 2017. *Helter-Shelter: Security, Legality, and an Ethic of Care in an Emergency Shelter*. Toronto: University of Toronto Press.

Ransom, Janet. 1993. "Feminism, Difference, and Discourse: The Limits of Discursive Analysis for Feminism." In *Up Against Foucault: Explorations of Some Tensions between Foucault and Feminism*, ed. Caroline Ramazanoglu, 123–46. London: Routledge.

Raymond, Janice. 1994. *The Transsexual Empire: The Making of the She-Male*. New York: Teacher's College Press.

–. 2015. "An Interview with Janice G. Raymond." 7 August. http://www.radfemcollective.org/news/2015/8/7/an-interview-with-janice-g-raymond.

Rose, Nikolas. 1996. "Governing 'Advanced' Liberal Democracies." In *Foucault and Political Reason: Liberalism, Neo-liberalism and Rationalities of Government*, ed. Andrew Barry, Thomas Osborne, and Nikolas Rose, 37–64. Chicago: University of Chicago Press.

–. 1999. *Powers of Freedom: Reframing Political Thought*. Cambridge: Cambridge University Press.

–. 2000. "Government and Control." *British Journal of Criminology* 40: 321–39.

Rose, Nikolas, and Peter Miller. 1992. "Political Power Beyond the State: Problematics of Government." *British Journal of Sociology* 43 (2): 173–205.

Rose, Nikolas, and Mariana Valverde. 1998. "Governed by Law?" *Social Legal Studies* 7 (4): 541–51.

Rose, Nikolas, Pat O'Malley, and Mariana Valverde. 2006. "Governmentality." *Annual Review of Law and Social Science* 2: 83–104.

Royal Canadian Mounted Police (RCMP). 2014. *Missing and Murdered Aboriginal Women: A National Operational Overview*. https://www.rcmp-grc.gc.ca/en/missing-and-murdered-aboriginal-women-national-operational-overview. Last viewed 19 May 2020.

Sangster, Joan. 1999. "Criminalizing the Colonized: Ontario Native Women Confront the Criminal Justice System, 1920–60." *Canadian Historical Review* 80 (1): 31–62.

–. 2001. *Regulating Girls and Women: Sexuality, the Family and the Law*. Oxford: Oxford University Press.

Sawicki, Jana. 1991. *Disciplining Foucault: Feminism, Power and the Body*. New York: Routledge.

–. 1996. "Feminism, Foucault, and 'Subjects' of Power and Freedom." In *Feminist Interpretations of Michel Foucault*, ed. Susan Hekman, 159–78. University Park: Pennsylvania State University Press.

–. 2013. "Queer Feminism: Cultivating Ethical Practices of Freedom." *Foucault Studies* 16: 74–87.

Scott, Joan. 1992. "Experience." In *Feminists Theorize the Political*, ed. Judith Butler and Joan Scott, 22–40. New York: Routledge.

SEED (Supporting Employment and Economic Development). 2014. http://seedwinnipeg.ca/.

Sevenhuijsen, Selma. 2004. *Citizenship and the Ethics of Care: Feminist Considerations on Justice, Morality, and Politics*. New York: Routledge.

Shantz, Laura, Jennifer Kilty, and Sylvie Frigon. 2009. "Echoes of Imprisonment: Women's Experiences of 'Successful (Re)integration.'" *Canadian Journal of Law and Society* 24 (1): 85–106.

Simpson, Leanne Betasamosake. 2017. *As We Have Always Done: Indigenous Freedom through Radical Resistance*. Minneapolis: University of Minnesota Press.

Smart, Carol. 1992. "The Woman of Legal Discourse." *Social and Legal Studies* 1 (1): 29–44.

Snider, Laureen. 2003. "Constituting the Punishable Woman: Atavistic Man Incarcerates Postmodern Woman." *British Journal of Criminology* 43 (2): 354–78.

–. 2014. "Making Change in Neoliberal Times." In *Criminalizing Women: Gender and (In)Justice in Neoliberal Times*, ed. Gillian Balfour and Elizabeth Comack, 268–89. Halifax: Fernwood.

Soper, Kate. 1993. "Productive Contradictions." In *Up Against Foucault: Explorations of Some Tensions between Foucault and Feminism*, ed. Caroline Ramazanoglu, 29–50. London: Routledge.

Stanko, Elizabeth. 1995. "Women, Crime, and Fear." *Annals of the American Academy of Political and Social Science* 539 (1): 46–58.

Statistics Canada. 2010. *2006 Aboriginal Population Profile for Winnipeg*. Ottawa: Minister of Industry. https://www150.statcan.gc.ca/n1/pub/89-638-x/2010003/article/11082-eng.htm.

Sudbury, Julia. 2005. "Introduction: Feminist Critiques, Transnational Landscapes, Abolitionist Visions." In *Global Lockdown: Race, Gender, and the Prison-Industrial Complex*, ed. Julia Sudbury, xi-xxviii. New York: Routledge.

Sullivan, Dennis, and Larry Tifft. 2005. *Restorative Justice: Healing the Foundations of Our Everyday Lives*, 2nd ed. Monsey: Willow Tree Press.

Taylor, Dianna. 2004. "Foucault's Ethos: Guide(post) for Change." In *Feminism and the Final Foucault*, ed. Dianne Taylor and Karen Vintges, 258–74. Chicago: University of Illinois Press.

Taylor, Dianna, and Karen Vintges. 2004. "Introduction: Engaging the Present." In *Feminism and the Final Foucault*, ed. Dianna Taylor and Karen Vintges, 1–11. Chicago: University of Illinois Press.

TFFSW (Task Force on Federally Sentenced Women). 1990. *Report of the Task Force on Federally Sentenced Women – Creating Choices*. Ottawa: Ministry of the Solicitor General.

Tomczak, Philippa. 2017. "The Voluntary Sector and the Mandatory Statutory Supervision Requirement: Expanding the Carceral Net." *British Journal of Criminology* 57 (1): 152–71.

Tronto, Joan. 1993. *Moral Boundaries: A Political Argument for an Ethic of Care*. New York: Routledge.

Turnbull, Sarah, and Kelly Hannah-Moffat. 2009. "Under These Conditions: Gender, Parole and the Governance of Reintegration." *British Journal of Criminology* 49 (4): 532–51.

Urban Aboriginal Peoples Study. 2011. *Urban Aboriginal Peoples Study: Winnipeg Report*. Toronto: Environics Institute.

Veracini, Lorenzo. 2010. *Settler Colonialism: A Theoretical Overview*. Basingstoke: Palgrave Macmillan.

Vintges, Karen. 2012. "Muslim Women in the Western Media: Foucault, Agency, Governmentality and Ethics." *European Journal of Women's Studies* 19 (3): 283–98.

Walgrave, Lode. 2002. "From Community to Dominion: In Search of Social Values for Restorative Justice." In *Restorative Justice: Theoretical Foundations*, ed. Elmar Weitekamp and Hans-Jurgen Kerner, 71–89. Portland, OR: Willan Publishing.

Weedon, Chris. 1997. *Feminist Practice and Poststructuralist Theory*. Cambridge: Blackwell.

Welsh, Megan. 2019. "How Formerly Incarcerated Women Confront the Limits of Caring and the Burdens of Control amid California's Carceral Realignment." *Feminist Criminology*, 14 (1): 1–26.

Wesley, Mandy. 2012. *Marginalized: The Aboriginal Women's Experience in Federal Corrections*. Ottawa: Public Safety Canada.

Whiteford, Martin. 2010. "Hot Tea, Dry Toast and the Responsibilization of Homeless People." *Social Policy and Society* 9 (2): 193–205.

Wodak, Ruth. 2001. "What CDA Is About: A Summary of Its History, Important Concepts, and Its Developments." In *Methods of Critical Discourse Analysis*, ed. Ruth Wodak and Michael Meyer, 1–13. London: Sage.

Wolfe, Patrick. 1999. *Settler Colonialism and the Transformation of Anthropology: The Politics and Poetics of an Ethnographic Event*. London: Cassell.

Wood, Linda, and Rolf Kroger. 2000. *Doing Discourse Analysis: Methods for Studying Action in Talk and Text*. Thousand Oaks: Sage.

Woolford, Andrew, and Amanda Nelund. 2013. "The Responsibilities of the Poor: Performing Neoliberal Citizenship within the Bureaucratic Field." *Social Service Review* 87 (2): 292–318.

–. 2019. *The Politics of Restorative Justice: A Critical Introduction*, 2nd ed. Halifax: Fernwood.

Woolford, Andrew, and Amelia Curran. 2011. "Neoliberal Restructuring, Limited Autonomy, and Relational Distance in Manitoba's Nonprofit Field." *Critical Social Policy* 31 (4): 583–606

Woolford, Andrew, and Robert Ratner. 2008. *Informal Reckonings: Conflict Resolution in Mediation, Restorative Justice and Reparations*. New York: Routledge-Cavendish.

Young, Iris Mario. 1994. "Punishment, Treatment, Empowerment: Three Approaches to Policy for Pregnant Addicts." *Feminist Studies* 20 (1): 32–57.

Zehr, Howard. 2002. *The Little Book of Restorative Justice*. Intercourse, PA: Good Books.

Index